BILLY GRAHAM

*A Life
Well Lived*

Sam
Wellman

BARBOUR
PUBLISHING

Published by Barbour Publishing, Inc., P.O. Box 719, Uhrichsville, Ohio 44683, www.barbourbooks.com

Our mission is to publish and distribute inspirational products offering exceptional value and biblical encouragement to the masses.

 Member of the
Evangelical Christian
Publishers Association

Printed in the United States of America.

Contents

Billy Graham, age eighty-eight, during the dedication of the Billy Graham Library in Charlotte, North Carolina, May 31, 2007.

Introduction

One of the great things about God is that He can, and very often does, use people of very ordinary backgrounds to accomplish extraordinary things.

William Franklin Graham Jr.—most of the world knows him better as "Billy"—is a great example of this truth.

Billy was born on November 7, 1918, to William Franklin and Morrow Coffey Graham. Billy, the first of four Graham children, grew up on a family dairy farm near Charlotte, North Carolina. His father was a successful farmer and businessman who believed in Jesus, the Bible, family, and the Protestant Work Ethic—and he did his best to instill those values in all of his children.

From an early age, Billy was no stranger to hard work. He grew up in a time when farm kids worked with their fathers and the hired hands almost as soon as they could walk. "He's up at four o'clock," Billy's mother said. "He goes right out with the men to do the milking." In addition to milking the cows, Billy fed chickens and goats and took care of other tasks.

Billy liked the cows, and they seemed to like him. This mutual affection helped Billy become an expert milker, something his father bragged about when Billy was just six years old. "Billy Frank can milk a cow faster than any six-year-old in North Carolina," his dad said. "The plain truth is he can already milk a cow pert'near as fast as a man."

Truth be told, Billy didn't become proficient at milking because he liked the task but because he wanted to get it over with. More important was getting on with things a kid living in the country enjoyed—and there was always plenty to do.

Every day seemed chock-full of school and work and fun for Billy. And then there was church.

Both William and Morrow Coffey were strong Christians who regularly took the family to the Associate Reformed Presbyterian Church. They also read the Bible and prayed at home. Billy's mother helped him memorize Bible verses and said every morning at the breakfast table, "Maybe today will be the day when the Lord comes again." Though there was a deep longing in her voice, Billy wasn't sure he wanted that to happen just yet. There was still so much he wanted to do.

There comes a time when every young man has to make his own decision about God.

Billy's parents did everything they could to make sure their children knew and feared God and loved His written Word, the Bible. But there comes a time when every young man has to make his own decision about God. . .when he has to make the faith his parents tried so hard to instill in him his very own.

That's where this book's real story—the story of a farm kid from an ordinary setting growing up to do extraordinary things for God—begins.

1
A Changed Boy

Billy's father, Frank, was grimmer than ever. Something bad had happened at the bank. Billy would have asked him, but he knew his father was not a complainer. Besides, he never said more than a few words, except when he prayed after supper. So Billy asked his mother.

"Yes," she sighed. "We lost all our money at the bank. Everybody did. Reckon some kids will be dropping out of Sharon High School soon enough. But not you, Billy. We have four hundred regular customers, and most of them will keep paying us. Folks with kids won't give up their milk. And besides, what did the Lord tell us?"

"Watch out! Be on your guard against all kinds of greed; a man's life does not consist in the abundance of his possessions."

"Luke 12," she said in a pleased voice.

Billy noticed no change at all. They had lost their savings, not

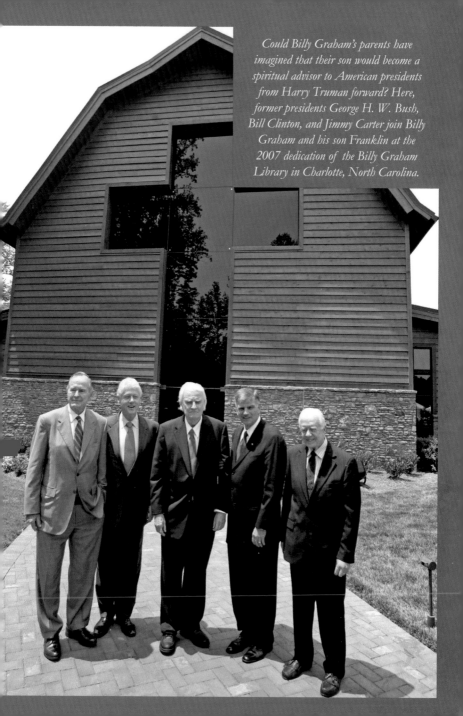

Could Billy Graham's parents have imagined that their son would become a spiritual advisor to American presidents from Harry Truman forward? Here, former presidents George H. W. Bush, Bill Clinton, and Jimmy Carter join Billy Graham and his son Franklin at the 2007 dedication of the Billy Graham Library in Charlotte, North Carolina.

their livelihood. And when Grandma Coffey died, Billy could accept that. She was pushing ninety. He had been right there when she rose up from her bed to cry out that she saw glory's blinding light and the outstretched arms of the Savior. She even saw angels and greeted her dear, departed Ben. Then she fell back on the pillow and died.

"She saw the Lord Jesus and heaven," gushed an aunt.

Even when his father had a terrible accident that same year, this earthly world didn't cave in on the Grahams. The dairy ran fine, thanks to his father's hired hands and big Reese Brown, the black foreman. Frank had been sawing a plank of wood with a circular saw and a knot flew off like a cannon ball, striking him in the mouth. From the nose down, his face was all smashed in. All his front teeth were gone, and that was the least of his injuries. Frank calmly walked over to Uncle Clyde's and had him drive him to the hospital. Once there, he lapsed into a fight with death.

By the following spring, Billy's father was back, but not as he was before. His thin, sad face was even droopier, even more woeful. He was even more active in the Christian Men's Club, which had existed ever since Billy Sunday's visit ten years earlier. The men in the club decided to hold several day-long prayer meetings. And, to Billy's amazement, one morning the men were parking cars by the house as he left for school. The men were gathering right in Frank Graham's pasture by a pine grove. Their wives were walking to the house to spend the day with Mother. And they were all still there when Billy came home after school to start his chores.

That night, his father was glowing. "What a day with the Lord! This fall we're going to build a tabernacle."

"Tabernacle!" blurted Billy.

"Steel frame and pine boards," said his father firmly. "We're going to have a real revival. Get us a real old-time preacher!"

Mother said, "I heard a man at your prayer meeting implored the Lord to let Charlotte give rise to a preacher who would spread the Gospel to the ends of the earth!"

"Maybe Charlotte is the end of the earth," said Billy with a smile. But his parents were not amused. Well, Billy didn't know who that man from Charlotte would be, but he was sure it wasn't him.

He was not enthused when he heard some preacher named Mordecai Ham was coming to Charlotte late that summer in 1935 to hold the revival meetings his father had talked about. How would he find time to go? He wasn't back in high school yet to start his junior year. But he worked hard on the farm. And when he wasn't working, he played baseball. When would he have time for Mordecai Ham, whoever he was?

Still, Billy went to the re-vival meeting with one of the tenant farmers, Albert Mc-Makin. Albert was almost ten years older than Billy and had been a star athlete at Sha-ron High School. When Billy

When Billy walked inside the tabernacle, he was stunned.

walked inside the tabernacle, he was stunned.

The tabernacle seemed magical. The darkness was lit by

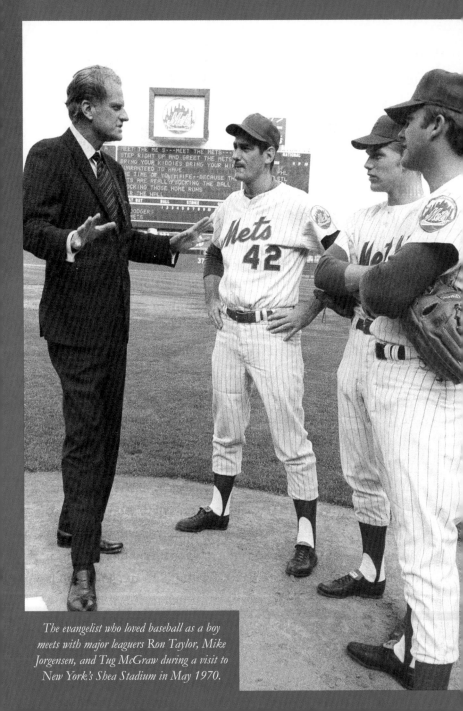

The evangelist who loved baseball as a boy meets with major leaguers Ron Taylor, Mike Jorgensen, and Tug McGraw during a visit to New York's Shea Stadium in May 1970.

dozens of high-swinging sunny bulbs. The air smelled of pine. The sawdust floor was primal but clean. There were already hundreds of folks sitting on benches and crates and chairs. And there was room for many, many more. Billy and Albert went down as close as they could get and sat right in the middle.

The tabernacle filled. There were so many people. Were folks so thirsty for the living water?

Mordecai Ham appeared on the stage. He was tall, fiftyish, with only a fringe of white hair and a thin white mustache. He wore rimless glasses. He had all the markings of a truly colorless man, but his face changed all that. It seemed to grow redder and angrier. Billy sat up tall so he wouldn't miss anything. He hoped this Dr. Ham spoke loud enough.

"You are a sinner!" bellowed Ham. He pointed right at Billy!

"Me?" gasped Billy. What had Billy done? Before the evening was over, Billy was shaken. He really did feel like a sinner.

Billy went back again and again, but he made sure he never sat in Dr. Ham's line of fire again. He joined the choir, which stood behind Ham. He was next to the two Wilson brothers, T. W. and Grady.

Every night Mordecai Ham ended his preaching by calling folks to the altar to accept Jesus as their Savior and be born again. Finally, one night after Dr. Ham invited sinners to the altar and the choir began singing, "Just as I am, without one plea except that Thy blood was shed for me," Billy felt the presence of the living Christ. Was Jesus telling him to go to the altar? Billy resisted. He was already a Christian. He was baptized. Of course he didn't remember it. He was just a baby. But he was Christian. Wasn't he? The choir started another hymn:

> *Almost persuaded now to believe;*
> *Almost persuaded Christ to receive;*
> *Seems now some soul to say,*
> *Go Spirit, go thy way,*
> *Some more convenient day,*
> *On thee I'll call. . . .*

Billy glanced at Grady Wilson. Grady was very troubled. "I thought I was already saved," he stammered. "Maybe I'm not."

Billy gaped as Grady lurched forward to the altar. As the choir sang the last words of the hymn "Almost—but lost!" Billy found himself trudging to the altar, head down, suddenly painfully self-conscious of his gangly height. Afterward, father Frank was suddenly beside Billy. His father put his arm around him, tears in his eyes. So his sad-faced father wanted Billy to be born again all along and never once pestered him about it. God would make it happen or not happen. And God made it happen.

"I'm a changed boy," Billy told his mother that evening.

Billy was slightly uneasy, though. He was born again, but where were the fire and joy? It had been nice in the tabernacle when his father put his arm around him. And it was nice to see how thrilled Mother was when she heard about it. But in his bedroom later, to the sound of his brother Melvin snoring, he felt tremendously disillusioned and burdened. Billy felt his imperfections now magnified. Maybe he didn't really understand what living in Christ meant.

But weeks later his mother said, "You've calmed down, Billy. You seem more tuned in to other people. I know you have always loved other people, but sometimes you were moving too fast."

Billy *was* changed. And not everyone appreciated it. He had to remind himself constantly not to be

Some kids started calling him the "Preacher Boy."

self-righteous because lately he had meddled with kids at school, telling them right out if they did something wrong. Some kids started calling him the "Preacher Boy." And it was not ribbing but carried a small niggling hatred. He was learning that some folks wanted their religion watered down or not at all.

His last two years of high school were a struggle between the old, fun-loving Billy and the new, self-righteous Billy. Sometimes the two Billys were all tangled together, like the time he saw some friends bullied in the parking lot after a basketball game. A fistfight broke out, and Billy hurled himself into their midst, but hardly as a peacemaker. He hit one boy over the head with a bottle, drawing blood. The old Billy was satisfied afterward that he had stuck by his friends. But the new Billy prayed for forgiveness later that night.

Billy began preaching to the younger children on the farm,

including toddling sister Jean. It seemed a delightful game, inspired by Mordecai Ham. Completely spellbound by the power he had witnessed in Mordecai Ham, he impulsively went to Belk's Department Store in downtown Charlotte and began preaching on the sidewalk. He waved his arms and jabbed his finger at sinners as they fled past him. Afterward, he had to admit his evangelizing was a dismal failure as far as he could tell. But, strangely, he wasn't embarrassed or sorry.

On the farm, the family started talking about Billy being a preacher. His father was not pleased. He had planned on Billy working the dairy farm full time after high school, but now Billy would have to continue on in some college, which cost money. But his mother was pleased. Frank was only forty-six. He didn't need Billy that bad. And though there wouldn't be enough money for a truly fine school like Wheaton College, which cost an astronomical six hundred dollars a year, she was sure they could afford some Christian school somewhere.

"Maybe Billy will be that preacher from Charlotte who spreads the Gospel to the ends of the world," said Mother.

"God willing." Billy's father looked pained to presume such a thing.

"T. W. Wilson went out west to Tennessee to that college run by Dr. Bob Jones," volunteered Billy. "He likes it."

"I never heard of it," said Mother.

"Don't you remember? Jimmy Johnson went there," said Billy brightly. Jimmy Johnson was a young itinerant preacher who had stayed with the Grahams. Billy thought he was an excellent preacher. "I would be a preacher in a twinkling if I could preach like Jimmy Johnson."

> "I would be a preacher in a twinkling if I could preach like Jimmy Johnson."

"What's it cost?" asked his father.

"Well, now you know T. W. couldn't afford much, Daddy."

"That's it then. It's Bob Jones," said his father, looking like he could make no better bargain than that.

Suddenly, Billy was out of high school with a diploma in his hand. What was he going to do for the summer? His quandary didn't last long. Albert McMakin had left the farm to sell Fuller brushes door to door. He invited Billy and the Wilson brothers to come to South Carolina that summer and sell brushes.

"But I thought you were going to help me on the farm this summer," said Billy's father.

"I can save up money for college this way, Daddy," gushed Billy.

"You'll be back in two weeks," scoffed Uncle Clyde.

On that encouraging note, Billy left with the Wilson brothers to go to South Carolina.

2
The Evangelists

Billy opened his case, found one of his cheapest Fuller brushes, and knocked on the door of his first potential customer. The door opened. An exasperated face appeared in the doorway. "Yes?"

"I'm Billy Graham, ma'am. Your Fuller Brush man. I'd like to give you a free brush today. . . ." He held out the brush. "All you have to. . ."

"Thanks, sonny." The woman snatched the brush out of his hands and slammed the door.

"Say, wait just a cotton-picking minute. . . ."

Billy learned fast. At the next house, he said the same words, but he took his sweet time digging in the case for the free brush. Never again did a customer get a free brush without hearing an unstoppable avalanche of words. And Billy made sure his customer was blinded by his smile. Like everything Billy did outside of school, he threw himself into it heart and soul. He began to sell

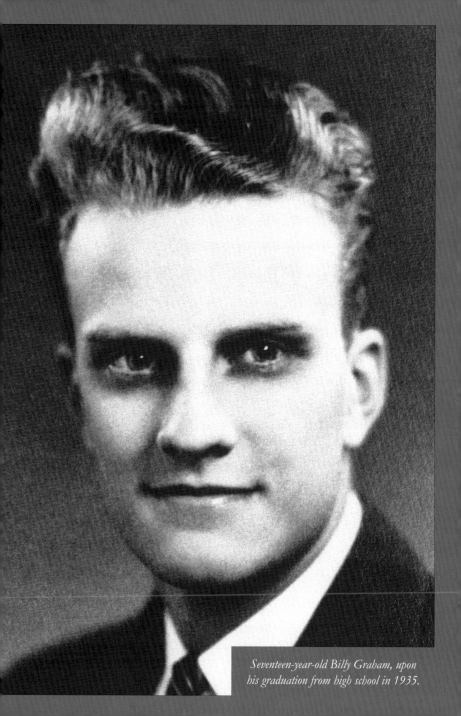

Seventeen-year-old Billy Graham, upon his graduation from high school in 1935.

brushes left and right.

After a few weeks, Billy was clearing fifty dollars a week after expenses. But he didn't save much of it. Billy liked nice clothes, and he loaded up on gabardine suits and hand-painted ties. And, of course, a salesman needed several pairs of comfortable shoes—nice saddletops, too, not clogs. At the end of the summer, he would have one fine wardrobe.

That summer, Billy crossed paths with Jimmy Johnson. Billy never missed a chance to hear Jimmy preach. One Sunday afternoon in Monroe, North Carolina, Jimmy took Billy and Grady Wilson to a jail. Facing the cells full of grumbling prisoners, Jimmy suddenly pointed at Billy. "I have a young fellow here who was just recently saved. Give our friends your testimony, Billy."

Billy was so surprised he dropped his case full of brushes. He began to nervously wring his yellow-piped green suit coat he had taken off because the jail was so hot and sticky. "Help me, Lord," prayed Billy. Hadn't he practiced a hundred times? "Get me started, Lord."

> "I was a sinner!
> I was no good!
> I forgot God!"

"I'm glad to see so many of you turned out," said Billy. Then he screamed, "I was a sinner! I was no good!" He punched the air. "I forgot God!" A weak "Amen" seemed to drift out of a dark, sweltering cell. "I didn't care about God! I didn't care about people!" He hunkered over now, then shot straight up with each sentence. Always the arms flailed. "Finally, I accepted Jesus!" His voice was whopping back off the walls, each word as loud and clear as a church bell. A few "Amens" made him louder yet. "Jesus brought me joy!" He felt like he could fly. Finally, he stopped, trembling in a state of joy he had never felt before. It would be a good while before the excitement wore off.

"So that's what preaching is really like," he gushed to Grady later.

All summer long, Billy sold brushes and evangelized. After summer was over, Billy's father drove the boys way out west to Tennessee. Billy and Grady were chomping at the bit. They would get this school of Bob Jones cooking. First, they would take over the freshman class. They hatched a plan. Billy nominated Grady for president of the class. Grady won the election. But when it came time for Grady to nominate Billy for an office, he found out officers couldn't nominate candidates.

At first Billy thought the school run by Bob Jones was wonderful. Jones was about as wide as he was tall, snowy-haired with a florid face. Somehow he preached out of the side of his mouth, and his voice was loud and mangled. Still, after a few weeks, Billy was disheartened. It wasn't the preaching he heard, but the regime of the students. Boys couldn't talk to girls. Mail was monitored. Billy felt like a prisoner, his impulsive energy piling up demerits at a record pace. For the first time in his life, he had trouble sleeping. Finally, he began to disintegrate, like some wild, wonderful jungle cat in a small cage.

Billy returned home for Christmas vacation, everyone thinking he had the flu he acted so miserable. He had to be dragged

Sixty-three years after Billy Graham realized his call to evangelism, he received an honorary knighthood for his life's work. Here, he speaks after a ceremony at the British Embassy in Washington D.C., December 6, 2001.

along in his father's brand-new green Plymouth when the Grahams drove south to visit his mother's sister in Florida. But at gasoline stops south of Jacksonville, Billy was now the first one out of the car.

"So this is Florida," he muttered and gawked. "Warm for December."

As they neared Orlando, he was leaping from the car. "Look at the palm trees!" His arms spread out. "Look. Flowers everywhere!" He punched the air. "Isn't this December?" He clapped his hands. "What a paradise!"

Soon after they visited his mother's sister in Orlando, they took a side trip to the west. East of Tampa in the midst of orange groves was the small town of Temple Terrace. The Grahams stopped to survey the Florida Bible Institute. Pale stuccoed buildings with red-tiled roofs overlooked tennis courts and a sprawling golf course.

"They say it was a former resort hotel and country club," said his mother casually. "It appears to be a fine institution to study God's Word. I read about it in *Moody Monthly.*" Then Billy realized his mother had engineered the whole Florida trip to show him another school. The Institute was deserted because of Christmas vacation, but Billy had no problem at all imagining himself striding across campus in balmy sunshine.

When he returned to Bob Jones's school, he tried to talk the Wilson brothers into coming with him to the Florida Bible Institute. They refused. Bob Jones was all they could afford. So Billy talked his friend Wendell Phillips into going with him.

Billy's father drove him to Florida in February 1937. Billy flourished like an orchid at Temple Terrace. The Institute had rules against smoking, drinking, "heavy" dating, but these were virtues nearly every one of these students had maintained all their lives, so it seemed there were no rules. Billy felt free.

Fun was encouraged at the Institute as well as hard work. Billy played tennis and golf, and he paddled canoes. The curriculum was no better than that at Bob Jones's school, he had to admit, but students were urged to practice preaching and given opportunities whenever possible. The word was out: a student had to be ever ready to preach. Billy polished four sermons he borrowed from a book, a common practice. He now had what he figured to be at least two hours of preaching in his heart. Who knew when he would be called? John Minder, a dean at the school and the director of the Tampa Gospel Tabernacle, took Billy with him on Easter vacation to a conference center in Jacksonville. And sure enough, Billy got his call: he was going to preach that very night!

The congregation at a small church near Palatka numbered about thirty. Billy got wound up and hammered out his four sermons in less than ten minutes. Dean Minder deftly filled in the remaining time. Billy felt miserable. Why couldn't he slow down and be like a real preacher? When they returned, Dean Minder asked him to be the youth director at the Tampa Gospel Tabernacle.

"Me?" asked Billy, still haunted by Palatka.

"Our youth group is small and discouraged, and you're just the man to energize them."

Billy threw himself into it with his usual energy. He remembered his final days at Sharon High School. Kids of high school age pulled away from him there. But he found these Tampa youths different. They were the cream. They were seeking God. They responded to Billy's loud, fervent prayers. And the group grew in number. Billy was thrilled that he could lead. Maybe he was cut out to serve God after all.

Life at the Institute was wonderful, the most glowing of his eighteen years. Then the last ingredient to his happiness was added: infatuation. This time the girl was Emily, whose family lived in Tampa. Emily was a dark-haired beauty, pious and talented. With sisters Inez and Pleasant, she sang gospel music far and wide. She had even performed on the radio. Billy was surprised by her interest in him.

> *Billy was thrilled that he could lead.*

And their romance began. He took Emily home with him the next vacation break. He began to sustain himself with thoughts about marriage. But then Emily dealt him a real blow: "I don't love you, Billy. I love someone else."

What was the purpose of all that heartache? What was God's purpose in having a young person crushed by such injustice? Was it to show that only the love of Christ and love from Christ were true?

Night after night, he lay awake in his dorm room, now taken to sleeping on the floor to ease his back pain, agonizing over his misfortunes and doubts. He brooded on and on, unable to sleep, wandering in lonely misery. Misfortunes had clouded his calling. His misery had evolved into doubts about being a preacher at all.

Finally, on a cool March night in 1938, he sat down on the eighteenth green with his back to the front door of the Institute. The veil lifted. Flickering in his mind were glimpses of rallies, throngs of folks spread before a platform higher than a throne. Yes, somehow he was going to be a small part of that.

Billy threw himself into Christ now. He prayed hours on end and read the Bible as he never had before. He was appointed assistant pastor of the Tampa Gospel Tabernacle, but that was not enough. He was willing to try anything to spread the Gospel. He became the preacher to a trailer park and preached to Cubans through an interpreter. He preached on the student radio station. Once he preached on a sidewalk in downtown Tampa, trying to save folks from going inside a sleazy bar, a certain step to hell. The bartender, discovering why business was slow, gave him one chance to leave then whacked him sprawling into the street.

Billy returned to Palatka. This time it was billed as his own revival. He was very bold. He asked fellow ministers to plug him now. Cecil Underwood was quoted in a local paper as saying Billy was "causing quite a sensation." Stoked by Underwood, the paper went on with flaming rhetoric that Billy led "the greatest meeting in the history of the church." Billy promoted himself all the time now. He sought publicity in newspapers and had modest handbills printed announcing his meetings.

Ministers around the area had their doubts. Billy was already a master at praying. More than anyone they had ever heard, he seemed to be actually talking to God. Yet his message was not novel. It was plain vanilla. The pointing finger: "You are a sinner. Christ died to pay for your sins. But you must accept Christ to be saved."

Billy knew what they were saying: he was colorful, but it was hard to see how anyone but the most backward hick would buy such a frantic message. But when Billy surrendered himself to Christ, it was all or nothing. This frenzied nonstop, sin-stomping preaching was Billy.

"I'm sure God wants me to preach this way," he told himself.

Still, results were what counted, weren't they? Could he or could he not bring sinners to Christ and salvation? So far he had never made the call to the altar. That was done by the presiding pastor. If Billy couldn't bring folks to Christ, he might as well give it all up and go back to the dairy or sell brushes. There was only one way to get the answer. He had to test himself with real people. Just the thought of it made him sweat.

> *This frenzied nonstop, sin-stomping preaching was Billy.*

3
Wheaton

When the night for his first altar call finally came, Billy gnawed at his fingernails, sick with worry. He had prayed all afternoon for God's help. In Venice, sixty miles south of Tampa, he was going to preach at a store-front church, a converted meat market.

One hundred people were in the congregation to listen to him preach. Heart pounding, he began. As he preached, he felt very strong. He really felt as if the Holy Spirit was helping him. Arms flailing and words exploding like gunfire, he delivered the Gospel. At the end of his sermon, when Billy invited them down to the altar to accept Christ, his heart was in his mouth.

He stood, hands clasped, eyes down, waiting in sweaty humility. Surely at least one would come. Oh please, God, just one. All he wanted was one. He waited.

Slowly a man stood up then hesitated before slowly turning to the altar. Yes! He was coming forward. Oh, praise the Lord!

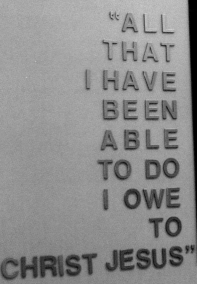

"ALL
THAT
I HAVE
BEEN
ABLE
TO DO
I OWE
TO
CHRIST JESUS"

Billy Graham

"All that I have been able to do I owe to Jesus Christ. Any honors I have received I
accept with a sense of inadequacy and humility and I will reserve the right to hand
all of these someday to Christ, when I see him face to face. Because I'm a servant,
not a master, I'm the servant of the King of Kings."

BILLY GRAHAM

...ter, and I don't claim to be a great
...l was one of those great
... the best

*Here is the secret to Billy Graham's success: a humble
acknowledgment that he was only a servant of Jesus
Christ. The sign is part of an exhibit at the Billy Graham
Training Center near Asheville, North Carolina.*

Another stood up and came forward.

Then another.

And another.

Soon they were rising so fast, Billy could no longer count. He wanted to weep. He wasn't worthy of such an outpouring. This was not about Billy's sermon. The sinners came to Christ because the Holy Spirit was working *through* Billy. Somehow God had blessed him, Billy Frank Graham, with the power of the Holy Spirit!

"Thirty-two came to the altar," said one of the local churchmen later. "In all my years, I never saw that many come to the altar in one meeting. You have something special, Billy Graham. But what?"

By early 1940, Billy was nearing graduation from the Institute. What was he going to do now? He could stay with the Tampa Gospel Tabernacle. He could get plenty of other preaching, like he already had. Maybe even a full pastorship would be offered to him.

In the meantime, he was still a student, doing all the menial things students did. One day he was caddying for two golfers named Elmer Edman and Paul Fisher.

Paul Fisher said, "We're from Wheaton, Illinois."

Billy gushed, "Where Wheaton College is located? What a co-incidence. My mother always dreamed of me going there."

Fisher set his jaw. "I heard your sermon at the Tabernacle. Very nice, Billy."

"Thank you, sir." Billy noticed Edman trying to stifle a smile.

"Need a bit more rounding," said Fisher. "Pretty heavy on the sin."

"I appreciate your advice," said Billy.

Billy knew Fisher was studying him to see if he was angry. Billy smiled. He really could take advice and did not take offense to criticism. Besides, Billy loved folks in general. Only injustice set him off.

Fisher went on, "My brother is the chairman of Wheaton College's board of trustees. Mr. Edman's brother is president of the college."

> *Billy loved folks in general. Only injustice set him off.*

"Wow," said Billy. "You must be proud of them."

Fisher said, "I want you to go to Wheaton, Billy."

"Can't afford it, sir."

"I'll pay your room and board for one year." Fisher looked at Edman. "Elmer?"

Edman said, "I'll pay your tuition for a year. After that, I expect you can get a scholarship. Truth is, we want Wheaton College to graduate Billy Graham."

In late summer 1940, Billy Graham, like every young man in America, went ahead with his plans but eyed Europe nervously. The continent was in the murderous grip of the Germans and Adolf Hitler's devilish Nazi party. English soldiers, the last real resistance on the continent, were overwhelmed at Dunkirk in France and chased back across the English Channel to England.

"President Roosevelt will keep us out of it," Billy's father said to him as he threw his luggage in the trunk of the Plymouth.

"Thank the Lord for that," replied Billy. Billy wasn't so sure, though. He had read a lot of history on his reading binges.

When Billy arrived at Wheaton College, He was twenty-two, an ordained minister yet a mere freshman. He majored in anthropology, which at Wheaton did not teach the student that every culture was different and that good and evil were relative but that every culture was essentially alike in its fallen state of sin, and the only answer was Christ.

As usual, Billy stretched his time to the limit. He got a part-time job moving furniture with a senior student, Johnny Streater.

"Say, Billy, my girlfriend has a friend I'd like you to meet," said Streater.

"I guess that's okay," said Billy politely.

So Johnny Streater introduced him to Ruth Bell. She was a second-year student, a daughter of missionaries in China. She was cool to Billy at first. Most girls did a double take, but not Ruth. She was looking for something else in a man. Billy immediately fell in love with her.

He thought about her all the time. But he had been burned before, and he was cautious. His interest in girls had been platonic, almost priestly. But Ruth Bell inflamed him. In his room in Professor Gerstung's home, he slept on the floor and prayed about her. He was not going to force the issue with her. He was going to leave it to God.

But after several weeks, he had to admit to himself that Ruth was not going to make the first move. So he nervously invited her to a performance of the *Messiah*. And while he waited an eternity for her answer, he realized his reluctance had not been in deference to God's plan but in fear of rejection. In all other matters, he knew a godly person carried out God's plan as best he could determine it and did not wait for God to intervene.

Ruth accepted!

The date with Ruth was both satisfying and disturbing. Ruth seemed compatible spiritually. She seemed very pleased to learn he didn't drink or smoke or dance. She seemed amazed that he had not seen one movie since he had received Christ under Mordecai Ham's preaching in 1935. The problem was that Ruth wanted to be a missionary. Yet Billy wrote his mother that very night that he had met the woman he was going to marry.

But the more he thought about Ruth Bell, the more troubled he became. How could her goals ever be reconciled with his? Could he rob this godly woman of her destiny? Once again he backed off. He saw Ruth at student prayer meetings but remained aloof. And finally, many weeks later, he received a letter from Ruth: an invitation to a party!

> *Billy wrote his mother that very night that he had met the woman he was going to marry.*

Over the months, they dated, usually going together to prayer meetings and sermons. Sometimes Ruth would talk of her childhood in China. Communist China was dark and terrible, and Ruth had witnessed some terrible things there.

Billy was still troubled by the separate paths he and Ruth seemed to be taking and prayed for guidance. Finally, he decided he was going to ask Ruth to marry him and let God sort the careers out.

When the students left Wheaton for the summer recess, Ruth still had not given Billy his answer. She was agonizing over it as much as he was. Billy knew after all his dilly-dallying, he had come on very strong. But a biblical marriage was the only kind of marriage for him.

Billy went to preach again in Tampa and received her answer by letter postmarked July 6, 1941.

"Yes!" he screamed.

He drove north to her grandmother Bell's house in the Asheville area. Ruth's parents were there, having just returned from China. Dr. Edman, the president of Wheaton College, asked Billy to replace him as an assistant pastor in the United Gospel Tabernacle. Naturally, Billy accepted.

Ruth soon visited the Grahams in Charlotte, wearing her sixty-five-dollar engagement ring. Billy's father now seemed well pleased with Billy's choices: for both a wife and a calling.

It seemed Billy and Ruth were moving to an inevitable marriage. But late that summer, Ruth's health failed. Dr. Bell thought she had malaria. He sent her to a sanitarium in Albuquerque with her older sister, Rosa. So it was no surprise to Billy when Ruth, in the clutches of depression, tried to break the engagement. That would pass, reasoned Billy.

On August 13, 1943, after three years of courtship, Billy married Ruth in a formal church wedding at Montreat, North Carolina. When the Billy Grahams returned from their honeymoon to

Illinois, it was to Hinsdale, not Wheaton. Billy started his pastorship at Western Springs more like a tornado than a shepherd. He herded his flock hard. He was a conservative evangelical through and through, but he persuaded his flock to change its denominational name to the Village Church so it could appeal to more people seeking a church. More and more people kept coming. And most important, they were drawn to the altar to accept Christ.

Opportunities seemed to seek Billy out. But, in fact, they found him because he was everywhere, opening doors. Each step Billy took seemed ten times higher than the last. Then he was approached with an offer from Torrey Johnson, pastor of the Midwest Bible Church. Like Billy, he had preached all around the Chicago area from time to time. But Johnson had gone far beyond that. He had learned to use the medium of radio.

> *Most important, they were drawn to the altar to accept Christ.*

Billy rushed home to Ruth with his news of Johnson's offer. This next step seemed a hundred times higher than anything before.

Billy Graham's live television debut: a screen shot of the ABC telecast of his June 1, 1957, Madison Square Garden crusade.

4
The Ministry Grows

"Torrey Johnson is overextended," Billy explained to Ruth. "He offered me his *Songs in the Night* radio program."

"But aren't you overextended, too? How will you find time?"

"I will. I have to. It's broadcast by WCFL—50,000 watts!"

"Then will you be heard all over the Chicago area?"

Billy laughed, but regretted it right away. After all, Ruth had grown up in China. "Ruth, 50,000 watts is as strong a transmitter as the law allows in America. My folks will hear me way down in Charlotte, especially since we broadcast late at night. We go on the air every Sunday night at ten fifteen."

"Your mind is made up and racing one hundred miles an hour."

"Maybe I can get that terrific bass baritone George Shea who sings on *Club Time* to sing hymns for our program. And do you remember that quartet of young women called the King's Karollers?"

"Where do you fit in?"

"Between songs." Billy smiled. "Don't you worry. We've got forty-five minutes of airtime to fill. You'll hear me plenty."

"Where do I fit in?"

"You can help with the scripts. Just like you help me with my sermons now. And I want you in the audience." Billy knew Ruth was struggling as a newlywed. Billy craved grapefruit, sausage, eggs, grits, and toast. Ruth liked to cook Chinese. Left on his own, Billy's idea of a perfect meal was to open three cans: Vienna sausages, tomatoes, and pork and beans. And Billy was sloppy. It was a blind spot with him. He could pile things in a corner for a year and it wouldn't bother him. It just didn't seem the least bit important. But he knew mostly it was his absence that irritated Ruth. He continued. "We'll broadcast right from the church."

"Now you're biting your nails. Why?"

"Our church will have to buy the airtime. And of course I could not ask such fine singers to perform regularly for no fee."

"Your congregation has done everything you've asked of them so far," said Ruth agreeably.

"It will cost about $150 a week."

"Whoa!" Ruth sat down. "One hundred and fifty dollars is about twice what you have at your discretion, isn't it?" she asked, shaking her head.

"Even that is not really at my discretion. We're trying to retire the mortgage."

The church elders were reluctant, too. The expense of the show seemed to be a surefire recipe for financial disaster. But Billy, in his eager, forceful way, persuaded them. On January 1, 1944, Billy welcomed listeners of *Songs in the Night* from "the friendly church in the pleasant community of Western Springs."

If ever proof was needed that his power was not from riveting blue eyes or a lion's mane of golden hair, the radio program proved it. Donations began to pour in to the church. It was not long until Billy ceremoniously burned the mortgage in a plate.

The radio experience helped Billy's preaching. He had to rely entirely on his voice and the message. But he didn't abandon his exaggerated gestures when he preached from the pulpit. He knew that a crowd seeing a preacher appreciated larger-than-life gestures.

Once again Torrey Johnson called on him. Torrey rented a concert hall. He wanted Billy to be his principal speaker at a rally for soldiers he called "Chicagoland Youth for Christ." Billy hesitated. He doubted Johnson could muster much of an audience. But that wasn't what really bothered him. It was one of Billy's few dark moments, one of those moments of crippling chest-tightening, dry-mouthed, lip-quivering doubt.

He accepted the invitation to preach. He walked out to face a concert hall that was packed with very tough, very cynical soldiers. He started to preach, still shaky as he watched some soldiers fidget. He was operating on faith that the Holy Spirit would take over. He did. When the talk was over, forty-two soldiers came to Christ.

Torrey Johnson's Chicago rally had been so successful, others followed, not only for soldiers but for young people in general.

And not only to those youth in the Chicago area, but young people nationwide. Eventually, Billy was preaching to crowds of ten thousand, and one time, to sixteen thousand. It happened so fast, he never had a chance to be overwhelmed by the immensity of what he was doing. Torrey Johnson had him traveling, too, making arrangements for the next rally and talking to participants.

By early 1945, Billy was so busy with Johnson's rallies, it was obvious he could no longer pastor the Village Church. The truth was that he had never seen the Western Springs calling as permanent.

So he left the church and began to work full time for Torrey Johnson. No one was more disappointed in the change of direction than Billy's parents. They faithfully listened to *Songs in the Night* on the radio. Ruth had encouraged the change. Was Billy going to be an evangelist or a pastor? She thought it was impossible to be both. But evangelism for Billy and Ruth was a double-edged sword. Preaching and planning Johnson's rallies for youth required him to travel constantly. And there was not enough money to pay for a wife's expenses, so Ruth could not travel with him. Billy was home so rarely, Ruth left Illinois to go live with her parents in Montreat.

Six hundred leaders showed up at Winona Lake in Indiana to formally start an international organization called Youth for Christ. To no one's surprise, Torrey Johnson was elected president. Billy became the single field representative for the new organization. Once again life changed drastically. He came to know airports everywhere. He lived out of a suitcase. But when he preached, he wore bright, outrageous colors to please young

Billy Graham at Montreat, in a photo taken May 1, 1957.

people. Billy was going to be twenty-seven that fall. He was known in the Chicago area to many evangelicals, and he was becoming known nationwide to evangelical leaders. Would he ever be known in his own home again?

He ached for home now. Ruth was pregnant. He tried to make amends to Ruth on sporadic visits to Montreat. Yet, somehow the Youth for Christ movement seemed always to be at hand.

Ruth gave birth to a daughter on September 21st. They named her Virginia after Ruth's younger sister, but Ruth nicknamed her GiGi, which was Chinese for "sister." Billy was not there. The die seemed cast. Billy was as ephemeral at home as a sea captain. The Youth for Christ movement was a national phenomenon by early 1946. By now the Youth for Christ organization was making its first efforts to enlist local clergy to counsel converts. That made a revival much more difficult. Advance planning was a very big part now, and that was Billy's job.

Also by 1946, Torrey Johnson decided it was time the organization truly became international. Teams left for Japan, Korea, China, India, Africa, and Australia. Another team left for England in March: Torrey Johnson himself, singer Stratton Shufelt, and the organization's two most dynamic speakers, Chuck Templeton and Billy.

English clerics were appalled by Billy. They had no clerics who preached in bright red bow ties. Their clerics did not stalk the platform, bending down, bolting upright, and flailing their arms. They had no clerics who spoke at the rate of 240 words per minute, never using an adjective or an adverb. His simple message of sin and salvation spattered the audience like machine-gun fire. There was no escape. Most stunning of all was the stream of sinners coming to the altar after he called them.

Even though the troupe had to create an agenda from scratch, they managed to speak to one hundred thousand British and Irish people in three weeks. And they made friends who would help them in future visits. They went on to Europe, where they had far more success creating a network of Youth for Christ groups among American occupation troops than converting the natives. The foreign languages and liberal theologies were a quagmire for Billy.

But he returned in the fall of 1946 to Britain and Ireland, this time for six months. His song leaders were Cliff Barrows and his wife. In the back of his mind, Billy felt like he was building a team. The itinerary had been arranged by a Scottish evangelist Gavin Hamilton. Later, Ruth was to meet Billy in London and accompany him for part of the trip. But Billy's first efforts were in Wales. It was so bitterly cold in Britain that winter that the Americans slept in their clothes.

By the end of his trip in March 1947, Billy and his troupe had spoken at 360 meetings, with major incursions into Manchester, Birmingham, Belfast, and London. And Ruth had traveled with him for a couple of weeks.

Billy wanted to work American cities like he had worked Birmingham. He started in Grand Rapids, Michigan. By the fall, he was to be in Charlotte. At Billy's citywide campaign in Minneapolis, eighty-six-year-old William Riley pestered him "like the persistent widow" to become president of Riley's Northwestern

Bible Schools. Billy refused. He had no time for that. Riley just wouldn't let up. So to silence him, Billy promised Riley to assume the role of presidency if anything happened to Riley within a year. Then he forgot about it.

The preparation for Charlotte was another of Billy's black moments. What if he failed in his own backyard? Even the Savior had been frustrated in his hometown of Nazareth. So Billy chewed his nails and spurred an advance campaign that went far beyond the usual billboards, bumper stickers, radio commercials, and placards in busses and windows. Billy had airplanes zooming over Charlotte, trailing banners and dropping leaflets. He gave daily press releases to thirty-one local papers. He advertised variety acts, even a race run by well-known miler Gil Dodds. He made sure Cliff Barrows and his wife were with him. He asked Bev Shea to sing for the campaign. He hired Grady Wilson to help out, even though it was Grady's brother, T.W., who evangelized fulltime for the Youth for Christ. Grady was married now, with his own ministry in South Carolina.

In eighteen services at Charlotte, they drew forty-two thousand people. And, as usual, Billy could persuade many of them to come to Christ. Billy was very pleased with his team of the Barrowses, Bev Shea, and Grady Wilson. He felt so good about his team now and his message that he began more and more to think about going out on his own to evangelize.

Then on December 6, 1947, while he was evangelizing for Youth for Christ in Hattiesburg, Mississippi, he got a phone call. After he listened to the voice, Billy had to sit down, stunned.

5
Crusading

Billy was shocked. He called Ruth. "William Riley died."

"May he rest in peace." Ruth sighed. "You promised."

Since spring 1945, Billy had traveled to forty-seven states for Youth for Christ. He had flown more than two hundred thousand miles. He didn't have time for his own family, yet he had promised William Riley. In a daze, Billy headed to Minneapolis to become the youngest college president in America. He was twenty-nine.

Like every job he did, he threw tremendous energy into it. He forged ahead with no less a goal than making Northwestern another Wheaton College. And he leaned on Grady Wilson's brother, T. W., to take over as administrator. T. W. refused at first, but Billy harangued him as persistently as William Riley had harangued him. He phoned him eight days in a row. Finally, T. W. took the position.

With T. W. installed, Billy became an absentee president. He

Billy Graham would circle the globe to preach his Gospel "crusades"—but he would also serve as America's pastor. Here, he speaks at a memorial service following the 1995 bombing of the Alfred P. Murrah Federal Building in Oklahoma City.

refused any salary and went on with his evangelizing. He would return to Minneapolis often enough to see that the Northwestern Bible Schools flourished, but he had more trips planned for England. And the chemistry of the new team he had assembled for the Charlotte crusade excited him. Split between the Bible school, his family at Montreat, and Youth for Christ, Billy knew 1948 was going to be hectic.

In Montreat, he bought a house across the street from Ruth's parents. It was obvious she could no longer cope in one upstairs bedroom of the Bell home.

As Billy drew away from Northwestern more and more, he realized he wanted to evangelize away from the Youth for Christ organization, too. He had great persuasion with youth. Somehow he could mellow the most rebellious young people with one or two corny jokes. It was a remarkable gift, because Billy wasn't funny. It was his unfunny way of telling a joke that was funny, and somehow it endeared him to listeners. But now Billy wanted to offer older people salvation, too.

"Or is it the influence of Chuck Templeton?" Billy grumbled to himself.

Charismatic Chuck Templeton was giving up evangelizing altogether. He had been accepted at Princeton Theological Seminary, and he tried to pull Billy away, telling him he had stopped growing intellectually and his pulpit theology was literal and simple-minded. Billy respected Chuck Templeton very much, and Templeton's new rationalism confused him. He couldn't answer Templeton's erudite criticisms of the Bible. At times he was really tempted to join Templeton at Princeton.

In November 1948, somewhat shaken by Templeton's defection, Billy called his closest friends together: Cliff Barrows, Bev Shea, and Grady Wilson. The team was evangelizing in Modesto, California.

"Gang," said Billy, gnawing on a fingernail, "we are on the brink of something bigger, I think. But we can't stop improving. Let's all go to our rooms and list all the things that are *wrong* with evangelism. Then we'll get together and discuss our lists and what to do about them."

So they tried to list their own flaws. When they compared lists, they were surprised how similar they were. One problem was the loose way they handled money. There must be no suspicion that they were lining their own pockets. They decided all offerings must be handled by a committee of the local clergy who invited them. The next problem was sexual temptation. They resolved with much prayer to avoid *all* situations that would put them alone with a woman, even something as innocent as a ride to the airport. The next problem was the common perception that they exaggerated their crowds. In the future, they would take police estimates even though they tended to be on the low side. Another problem was the perception that they exaggerated the number who came to the altar. They would admit right up front many of those coming to the altar were volunteers who were supposed to counsel

> *There must be no suspicion that they were lining their own pockets.*

the converts. They must study the cards the converts filled out and release accurate numbers. In fact, those who came to the altar were really not all converts. Some were just curious. Billy and his team would no longer call them converts. In the future they would call them "inquirers." Another problem was that evangelists in the past attacked the local clergy. They would guard against undermining the authority of local pastors.

Thus armed with this "Modesto Manifesto," the team continued its evangelizing. They had great successes and a few failures, too. Sometimes the failure was in traveling. Once in Canada, Billy almost died in a plane landing in a blizzard. That very same night, he was mistakenly identified as a fugitive and arrested. A few incidents like that almost soured Billy on traveling.

The year 1949 was a strange one for Los Angeles. In January it snowed heavily; the downtown area recorded the coldest temperature in its history: 28 degrees Fahrenheit. Even in September, when the air should have been warm and dry, it was cool and rainy. It made the extreme preparation for Billy's Greater Los Angeles Revival seem brilliant in hindsight. For three weeks the crusaders hoped to pack six thousand people six nights a week and twice on Sunday into Billy's "Canvas Cathedral"—a three-spired Ringling Brothers Circus tent—downtown on the corner of Washington and Hill streets. Armin Gesswein and Edwin Orr had labored mightily for nine months. They had organized eight hundred prayer groups to pray for the success of the revival. Dawson Trotman trained counselors to assist those who were to come to the altar. Cliff Barrows recruited a top-notch choir and singing groups.

The campaign had the support of more than 250 local churches as well as the mayor. Local celebrities were recruited, including Stuart Hamblen, a talented singing Texan with a daily radio program called *Cowboy Church of the Air*, but also with a reputation for living the good life. He was a drinking buddy of Hollywood movie stars like John Wayne.

When Billy went on Hamblen's show before the revival started, he was surprised to hear Hamblen blurt, "I'm going to be there, too!"

Most important to Billy's sense that all would go well was the rest of the team: Grady Wilson, Cliff Barrows, and Bev Shea. Grady was Billy's sidekick and jack-of-all-trades. He could organize prayer groups, preach if Billy got sick, tell funny stories, or cook breakfast. White-suited, halfback-burly Cliff, swinging his trombone, bounced through the singing like a cheerleader. Balancing Cliff or a local singing group was baleful dark-suited Bev Shea, who sang two hymns in somber reverence. Dignified Bev always preceded Billy's sermon to set the right tone. Since they had embraced a greater audience than youth only, Billy had toned down the service so that it was more a church service than a loud, colorful show.

His gaudy clothing was gone. He tended to wear dark suits more often, always with a handkerchief blossoming from the breast pocket. Billy started with a passage from the black Bible he clutched. "The Bible says. . . ," he would bellow, borrowing an old evangelist's phrase, before he went on to quote scripture. Then began his ringing denunciation of those who disobeyed God's Word and the dreaded consequences. He wore a lapel microphone now, so he could be heard in the farthest corners. He still stalked the platform, cracking out honeyed southern words like pops of lightning. He locked his eyes on several hundred people at once. When he had them squirming, it was time for a change of pace. He would soften his tone for a while or move on to lambaste another segment of his audience. Billy hammered through the list of sins: materialism, alcoholism, adultery, suicide, stealing, cheating, divorce, greed. But he never forgot to be current. That is what it took to convince many

> *He locked his eyes on several hundred people at once.*

skeptics that the Bible was relevant, even though new evils plagued man: rationalism, godless Communism.

And if any sinner assumed the dark suit had mellowed Billy into a detached saint, he was wrong. Stuart Hamblen quickly found that out. During the second week, Billy pistoled his finger in Hamblen's direction and snapped, "There's a man in here leading a double life!" The next night he leveled his finger at Hamblen again. "There's a phony in here tonight!" After that night, Hamblen refused to attend.

After three weeks it was customary to extend the crusade in Los Angeles if success merited it. Billy's success had been marginal. And the novelty was wearing off. The crowds were beginning to thin. Except for the greater expense he extracted from his hosts, he had enjoyed no more distinction than previous revivalists. But it was by no means a flop either, and the local committee asked him to decide himself if he wanted to extend the crusade. Billy had never extended a crusade before, no matter how successful, so to some on the team the gesture from their hosts was rather hollow.

"I'll put out a fleece," Billy said somewhat nervously Saturday, just one day before their last scheduled service. He was alluding to the story of Gideon in the book of Judges. One night Gideon put out a fleece on the threshing floor and asked God to give him a sign. If in the morning the fleece was covered with dew, yet the floor around it was completely dry, that would be a sign from God.

"But what is your fleece, Billy?" asked one of his contingent.

"It has been unseasonably cold or rainy ever since we got here. We'll see if the weather changes."

The weather had been cool every day. Billy's gesture, too, seemed hollow. Yet on Sunday, the air was uncomfortably warm inside the tent. Billy announced the revival would continue.

Billy called Louis Zamperini to the altar. In the 1930s, Zamperini had been a world-class distance runner, widely publicized for tearing down one of Hitler's swastikas at the 1936 Olympics. During the war as a combatant, he was adrift in a life raft for a month and a half in the Pacific. Then he survived a Japanese concentration camp. But eventually his great courage failed him. Until the Lord saved him under Billy's preaching, he found his courage in a liquor bottle.

Success snowballed. Not long after Zamperini testified on the platform, another man came to the altar. Of course the man didn't really believe Billy could save him, but he thought it wouldn't hurt to try. And the man came to the altar, reborn.

Former gambler Mickey Cohen, now a Los Angeles florist, poses by a Billy Graham poster advertising a 1957 New York City revival.

He was Jim Vaux, a henchman for the czar of the Los Angeles underworld, Mickey Cohen. Billy even met secretly with Cohen himself, who was curious about the power of this hawk-eyed evangelist. Their meeting was leaked to the press, probably by Cohen himself, who loved publicity.

"You've been used," commented one of Billy's friends.

"We may need a larger tent," replied Billy, gnawing his fingernails. "I need to call Armin Gesswein. This is getting awfully big awfully fast now."

Celebrities like Gene Autry and Jane Russell began to attend the revival. Suddenly, the crusade was being touted in two Los Angeles newspapers, the *Herald* and the *Examiner*, with full-page stories and photos of Billy haranguing the crowd like John the Baptist. Both Los Angeles newspapers were owned by the old friend of the Youth for Christ: William Randolph Hearst. It only became apparent to the revivalists in Los Angeles that Hearst was running the story in his papers across the rest of the country when reporters from the national magazines *Life*, *Quick*, *Newsweek*, and *Time* showed up.

But inside, he was disconcerted because he was running out of sermons. Ruth was with him now. She had come in the third week, leaving GiGi with her parents and Anne with her sister, Rosa. She had planned to leave Los Angeles with Billy at the end of the week. Now she stayed through the extension, helping him every way she could.

The Canvas Cathedral overflowed on his last meeting, on November 20th. The seating inside had been expanded to nine thousand. The crowd overflowed into the street as it had several times recently, blocking traffic. In eight weeks, Billy had drawn 350,000 listeners, of which three thousand had come to the altar to inquire. Local churches helping him had swollen to seven hundred. Everything seemed magnified. One cleric suggested Billy start a church in Los Angeles.

> *In eight weeks, Billy had drawn 350,000 listeners.*

"It will be kind of nice to get away from all the hubbub for a while," said Billy to Ruth as they boarded the train to Minneapolis the next day. But the train was no refuge. Everyone seemed to know him now. The conductor and porters treated him like a celebrity. At Kansas City, reporters rushed inside the train, asking questions and popping flashbulbs.

In Minneapolis, as Billy addressed his amazed cohorts at Northwestern Bible School, he was suddenly overwhelmed by what had happened in Los Angeles. He couldn't continue. He had to sit down, struck speechless.

An estimated fifty thousand people attended
Billy Graham's rally on the historical
Boston Common, April 23, 1950.

6
A New Awakening

It was more than the immensity of events catching up with Billy that robbed him of his tongue. He was run down, and his doctor ordered him to rest one month.

"And rest I will," he agreed thankfully.

At Montreat, he played with four-year-old GiGi and eighteen-month-old Anne. And when the children tired him, the grandparents kept them across the street while Billy and Ruth had "quiet time." Once in a while, the success at Los Angeles would bubble up from his memory and overwhelm him. There was only one way for him to put Los Angeles in its proper perspective: to remember that he was a mere instrument of God's will.

"I know you're recovering now," commented Ruth one day.

"How do you know?" asked Billy.

"You're biting your fingernails, probably worrying about your next campaign."

"Boston?" said Billy breezily, but he was very worried.

Billy's team could not have picked a tougher city to evangelize. Boston was dominated by Catholics, and its Protestant clergy were so stodgy, they had refused to sponsor a Youth for Christ rally Billy had tried to hold there once. The initial reaction of the New England Evangelical Association to Billy's latest proposal for a revival was to have Billy come for one sermon on New Year's Eve. More adventurous clergy had prevailed. Billy was scheduled for ten days.

The first night Billy preached to six thousand at Mechanics Hall. When he invited them to the altar, his team held its breath. "One hundred and seventy-five," said their host, Harold Ockenga, slightly dazed. "In Boston?"

Enthused at such success, they announced an impromptu meeting the next afternoon. The only other notice of the meeting was in a few hastily amended Sunday morning church bulletins. Nevertheless, Billy preached to another six thousand with the same success. At the regularly scheduled meeting that night, two thousand had to be turned away. The next night they turned away seven thousand.

The Boston rallies grew. Billy was invited to open the state legislature with a prayer. Shifting from auditorium to auditorium now to accommodate the much larger than expected crowds, Billy finally found himself in his final meeting at Boston Garden,

At Boston Garden, the revivalists jammed sixteen thousand inside, with another ten thousand standing outside.

where the Celtics played basketball. The revivalists jammed sixteen thousand inside, with another ten thousand standing outside. Bostonians were singing hymns in the street.

On the train away from Boston, he told Ruth, "It seems like my heart is crying out to me to go back. The finale at Boston Garden was a sign that we were on the verge of some colossal new awakening. Folks were singing in the streets. There was great joy."

"Why can't we go back?"

"Too much on our schedule." But he had an ache in his heart as if he would regret not going back as long as he lived. Had he disobeyed God?

Billy preached for three weeks in Columbia, South Carolina. Willis Haymaker had done masterful advance work. He organized prayer groups and got local churches to block out certain nights so every meeting had the core of a good audience. Haymaker was the first to call the revivals a "crusade," implying it was an ongoing effort that would not end when Billy left town.

The governor of South Carolina, Strom Thurmond, backed Billy. As he had done in Boston, Billy went to the state legislature. But this time he gave a speech warning America not to backslide as the Jews did in the time of Isaiah. His crusade was a success, and again he could not believe the opportunities that came to him.

"The last meeting of the crusade is where?" Billy asked his hosts.

"University of South Carolina football stadium," was the answer. "It holds thirty-five thousand."

Billy was aghast. "Can we fill it?"

"Oh, you of little faith," cracked one of the contingent.

Billy had to laugh. He had used that very quote to win an argument a few days earlier. But why take such a chance? Did they have to push God to the limit? This success wasn't Billy's doing. Hadn't God done enough for one crusade? But it was too late. The stadium was news already.

All the while Billy strode to the platform for the finale, he praised God. Forty thousand people crowded inside the football stadium. Ten thousand were turned away. Billy preached about Noah and the flood as God's judgment. And there was a great flood of people who came to the altar.

He returned to New England. In spite of his worry over such success, he felt he had to seize the moment and be bold. To a crowd the Boston police estimated at fifty thousand, he urged President Truman to call for a day of national repentance as President Lincoln had done. And Billy outlined his own five-point plan for peace. The first three points were to maintain security through military, internal, and economic strengths. The fourth was to put aside all divisiveness and unite all races and creeds. His fifth was to have a moral and spiritual regeneration through repentance and faith in Christ.

No one could doubt Billy had risen to prominence when he received an invitation to visit the White House after the New England crusade.

"How should we dress?" Grady asked.

"What do you mean?" asked Billy. "Wear a dark suit and black shoes."

"But Truman is a casual guy. Haven't you seen pictures of him at Key West in his spiffy white bucks and loud Hawaiian shirts?"

"We can't wear Hawaiian shirts to the White House," argued Billy.

"What about white bucks?"

That seemed like a great idea. That would definitely break the ice. Billy enthused, "We could wear light summer suits, hand-painted ties, and white bucks. Let the president know we're down-to-earth folks—just like he is."

> *"Let the president know we're down-to-earth folks—just like he is."*

And that's how Billy, Cliff Barrows, Grady Wilson, and Jerry Beaven, the newest member of the team, dressed for the meeting at the White House with the single most powerful man in the world. They showed up well ahead of time and sat outside the Oval Office, squirming. Watchless, Billy asked his friends what time it was every few seconds.

Finally, they were taken into the office.

The bespectacled president greeted them, adding good-naturedly that he was a Baptist. Truman stood ramrod straight in a dark suit. As Billy began to preach for a national day of repentance, the president interrupted him impatiently. "I live by the Sermon on the Mount and the Golden Rule. I said I was a Baptist. . . ."

"Would it be all right if we prayed before we leave, Mr. President?"

"I don't suppose it could do much harm."

Billy put his arm around the president and delivered his message in prayer, as Cliff chanted, "Yes, do it, Lord," and "Amen."

Billy moved on to his Portland, Oregon, crusade. Things were happening at a feverish pace. Two friends of his ministry, Walter Bennett and Fred Dienert, were trying to negotiate a package for a weekly radio program with the ABC network. At first Billy was enthused. But when he realized the program would cost his organization seven thousand dollars a week, besides costing him hours and hours of precious time to prepare a flawless program, he balked. When the two men told him ABC wanted thirteen weeks guaranteed, or ninety-two thousand dollars, Billy almost fainted.

"The answer is no," he said. And now he avoided the two negotiators.

Billy had become more and more a captive of his popularity. It was difficult to walk about freely now. He spent more and more time in his hotel room when he was not preaching—like he did now in the Multnomah Hotel in Portland. Often he would still be in his room at noon, eating lunch delivered by room service, in his pajamas, and wearing a green baseball cap to keep his unruly hair matted down. Then, before he finally left to preach, he would eat a light meal with tea.

> *The crusade in Portland was another staggering success.*

The crusade in Portland was another staggering success. Each one seemed to get larger. In Portland, the block-square tabernacle of aluminum and wood held twelve thousand seats. Standing-room-only crowds reached twenty thousand. In six weeks he had preached to half a million people.

In the meantime, Bennett and Dienert pestered Billy like the persistent widow. Now they insisted he needed only twenty-five thousand dollars up front. Finally, he threw out the fleece. He would have been appalled if someone said he only did that when he wanted to kill a project, but when he announced the terms of this "fleece," it did seem that way.

"If the Lord wants me to do this, I will have the twenty-five thousand dollars tonight—before midnight."

Billy did not tell his audience about the radio opportunity *before* the love offering that night; he told them *after* the offering. And he told them in a low-key, almost halfhearted way that the radio program would require twenty-five thousand dollars and that if anyone wanted to encourage this kind of evangelizing, they could donate money after the service.

"Well, we can bury that idea," grumbled a follower.

Unbelievably, people lined up afterward, coming one by one to the table where Billy was sitting with Grady Wilson. Money poured into a shoebox: five dollars, loose change, twenty dollars, and an occasional lunker like a check for twenty-five hundred dollars. Billy sat there, completely trusting God, saying over and over, "God bless you. Thank you."

After the line was exhausted, Billy didn't count the money. He gave the shoebox to their host committee and left to eat a late supper. It was during the meal that the team learned they had raised $23,500.

"It's a miracle!" screamed one of the diners.

"It's not enough," said Billy. "The devil is tempting us."

They trudged back to the hotel. They picked up their mail at the desk and rode the elevator up to their rooms. Inside Billy's room, Grady sorted through the mail.

"Say!" blurted Grady. "This envelope has a pledge in it for the radio program. Somebody must have dropped it off at the desk after the meeting broke up. Two hundred and fifty bucks. . ."

Now all eyes were on the stack of mail.

Sweat popped out on Grady's forehead as he opened letter after letter. He was smiling all the while he read the letters out loud. A check fluttered out of one envelope onto the table. Grady's smile almost split his face. "Another check for the radio program. One thousand dollars."

"How much is that then? Anybody totaled it all up?" asked Cliff Barrows.

"Twenty-four thousand seven hundred and fifty," said Grady, now grumpy as he realized it was not enough. He pawed through the rest of the mail, opening letter after letter. Then he pulled a check from one letter and smiled.

"Bingo. Two hundred and fifty dollars." The total had reached exactly twenty-five thousand dollars!

Billy wanted to call the radio program *Deciding for Christ,* but Ruth volunteered *Hour of Decision*. The team preferred Ruth's name. *Hour of Decision* went on the air November 5, 1950, over 150 ABC stations. The first broadcast was from an actual revival in Atlanta.

After Atlanta, the *Hour of Decision* would typically open with the stirring "Battle Hymn of the Republic," followed by Cliff Barrows's introduction, which ended with "This is the *Hour of Decision!*"

> *"This is the Hour of Decision!"*

Then came Grady Wilson reading a passage from the Bible. Jerry Beaven would read the news. Bev Shea would sing a hymn to set a somber, respectful mood. Then came what everyone waited for: Billy Graham. Billy would start with a development in the news—breathlessly, dramatically, like famed radio personalities Walter Winchell and Drew Pearson. The resemblance ended there. Billy brought in the Bible and relentlessly hammered his audience, never faltering for a word. The listener got no relief from Billy's impending hell without Christ until he said, "Goodnight and may the Lord bless you," then drawled a honeyed "real good."

7
Peace with God

The money situation was getting complicated. Billy had to be incorporated now that so much money was pouring in. It was crucial that he stay clear of any suspicion of money-grubbing. He objected to calling his organization the Billy Graham Evangelical Association, but even Ruth insisted his name had to be in the title.

Within months, the number of radio stations carrying the *Hour of Decision* doubled. The Billy Graham Evangelical Association got larger and larger. With the commitments of weekly radio and never-ending citywide crusades, the demands were great. The BGEA, headquartered in Minneapolis, added people to write scripts and take care of a thousand details. Already Billy and his team were considering a television program and a weekly newspaper column.

The organization began compiling a mailing list of sympathetic supporters. "BGEA won't use the list to hound folks for money," vowed Billy. But it didn't hurt to keep supporters

His ministry produced many evangelistic motion pictures—and in 1989, Billy Graham received his own star on the Hollywood Walk of Fame. Friends and family gathered to commemorate Billy's fortieth anniversary in ministry.

informed of their opportunities and drop the gentlest reminder that evangelizing required money.

If 1950 wasn't momentous enough, Ruth gave birth to their third daughter on December 19th. The infant was named Ruth Bell but almost immediately got nicknamed "Bunny." Now GiGi and Anne, aged five and two, had a real-live doll.

In 1951, Billy was talked into sponsoring Christian films. He formed World Wide Pictures, which made two movies called *Mr. Texas* and *Oiltown*. He even had a premiere for *Mr. Texas* in Hollywood with Cecil B. DeMille in the audience. In spite of stinging criticism of the film as hopelessly amateurish, Billy just shrugged and prayed that their efforts would get better. He had no intention of abandoning this promising approach to spreading the Gospel. And the "star" of *Mr. Texas* drove about the country showing his film to whoever was willing to watch.

Billy also launched a weekly television show called *Hour of Decision*. The show aired stirring clips of his crusades. Other times, the show had Billy sitting in a comfortable chair as if in a home library and delivering a calm, reasoned, low-key message. Sometimes he would give rehearsed responses to questions.

Billy continued his citywide crusades. Independent of Youth for Christ, he had preached for three years to several million people in many American cities. The crusades were maturing, and Billy had stopped all love offerings. Now a man or a woman need bring nothing but their souls to the revival. His radio and television shows inspired money to pour in to the Minneapolis office, where it was all meticulously accounted for. Billy figured a several-week citywide crusade now required a quarter of a million dollars. But he had another iron-clad requirement—that he be invited by a solid majority of local churches who would wholeheartedly participate and offer volunteers.

But the crusades were far from perfected. They still needed improvement. One great need was follow-up. Far too many times, inquirers flooded to the altar, then waited in vain in a logjam for counseling. Finally, many walked away. Billy was a fisher of men who was letting his catches slide back into the sea. It took many appeals by Billy to get the best man in the country to train his counselors fulltime. But finally, he got Dawson Trotman, founder of the Navigators, a group unsurpassed in counseling one-on-one and nurturing the Word in a new Christian.

Another need was gnawing at him. He had always called everyone to the altar together, even calling out pointedly, "The ground is level at the foot of the cross. I want all white folks, all colored folks to come forward." Yet he was still setting aside sections for blacks, thoughtfully placing them in the shade or trying to soften their segregation with some other minor convenience. How could he approve of any form of segregation? But what would happen to his ministry in the South, where Jim Crow laws were still rigidly enforced.

Billy searched the scriptures, but not for the right or wrong of segregation. He knew in his heart segregation was not in Christ. But the Bible cautioned one to be wise in the worldly ways of men. White folks had to be won over gradually. Yes, he was committed to doing something about segregation, but it would be slow and cautious.

Billy mounted his crusade in Washington, D.C., in early 1952.

He was still refining the BGEA and at last resigned from the Northwestern Bible Schools. He had served them four years, much longer than he had promised William Riley.

Billy kept expanding his organization within America during 1952. In addition to his radio and television shows, he started a weekly newspaper column called "My Answer," in which he answered pressing modern problems with scripture. The answers were not ghosted; he would dictate an answer, which would be polished by a professional writer. Then Billy had to give that polished answer one last review.

There was serious talk of a book now. New York publisher Doubleday approached him. Naturally they wanted a bestseller. Billy wanted a down-to-earth explanation of the meaning of Christ—maybe like the popular C. S. Lewis book *Mere Christianity*, but in Billy's style, stressing a greater urgency to seek salvation. But how would Billy go about it? In his wildest daydream, he couldn't write like Lewis. Doubleday suggested he send an outline and his sermons he felt were relevant, and they could get an editor to put it all together. So Billy worked on it.

Only later did the book begin to take shape as Billy had envisioned it. The project took a huge turn after Ruth first received Doubleday's draft.

"Take a look at this," Ruth said to Billy.

"Oh, no. I can hear the exasperation in your voice."

It was the manuscript. The ghostwriter's superficial knowledge of the Gospel had made a hodgepodge of the proposed book. So Billy threw the manuscript away and sat down with Ruth to write a new one. Friends critiqued it, and they rewrote it again. It cost Billy a chunk of time, but he was very happy with the manuscript. The book was now truly his—and Ruth's. He mailed it to Doubleday, and they agreed to publish it late in 1953 as *Peace with God*.

In early 1954, Billy decided to go to England. Ike wished him well, and even Earl Warren of the Supreme Court led a prayer to wish him well.

"But the disheartened England of 1954 is not the England that won the Second World War," said a worried Ruth.

Billy knew Ruth was probably expressing the sentiments of her father, Nelson Bell, who was very savvy about international politics. And then Billy started to worry, too. Why was he going to England? His citywide crusades in America were always successful now. And the only facility they could find in London was lackluster Harringay Arena, right by a dog racing track in north London, in a neighborhood so run down many Londoners might be afraid to attend a crusade.

Ruth soothed him enough to remember two key ingredients to a good crusade, prayer and publicity, were working for his success already. He had eighteen thousand faithful in England praying for the crusade. The crusade had launched an advertising campaign in London so aggressive that thirty thousand posters were distributed. They had spent a staggering sum for the time: fifty thousand English pounds.

A confident Billy sailed with Ruth for England on the *United States* in February. But before the ship ever docked in England, he got word the British were up in arms over his frequent criticisms of Socialism, which he used almost interchangeably with Communism. Socialism was a respectable option in England. The Labour Party had governed for several years after the war, before conservative Winston Churchill became prime minister again. But more than that, cradle-to-grave Socialism was a sacred cow to the press. When the ship docked at Southampton and the team disembarked, a horde of twenty-five reporters and eleven photographers swarmed around them like angry hornets. Reports in the London newspapers were uncompromisingly vicious. Even the photographs of Billy were snide, one captioned: NO CLERICAL COLLAR, BUT MY! WHAT A LOVELY TIE!

The unrelenting hostility crippled Billy. The day of the first meeting, he had one of his darkest moments. He had violated his own maxim: don't go where you are not wanted. He had gambled and lost.

One of the team came to him in his hotel room not long before the meeting was supposed to start. "I just talked to folks at the arena, Billy."

"Great," said Billy, gnawing a fingernail, trying to keep his spirits high. "Are they turning people away yet?"

"A couple of thousand are there, Billy."

"It should be full by now," mumbled Billy. The arena held twelve thousand. Billy got up and stood by the window. "It's snowing."

The ride to the arena was somber. Next to the arena, the dog track was lit up and thronging with patrons. But the parking lot to the arena was almost empty. Billy trudged dejectedly inside the arena.

8
Europe

Inside the arena, Billy had to blink his eyes. "It's packed to the rafters! Oh God, forgive me," he prayed, "for not trusting You. This is Your glory, not mine. How did they get here so suddenly? And where are the cars?"

"These are Londoners," answered one of his hosts. "They came on the underground. Last minute, old chap. Quite suddenly."

"There are Senator Symington and Senator Bridges," gasped Billy. "I thought they weren't coming."

"Their dinner engagement is after your meeting," explained someone.

In the first sermon, Billy jabbed the air. "There's a hunger for God in London!"

And he was right. Londoners flocked to the arena day after day. One great innovation was originated by Stephen Olford, the Welshman who had already greatly influenced Billy. It was

The Grahams pose for photos before Billy sails for Europe on March 12, 1955.

dubbed "Operation Andrew," after the apostle who brought his brother Peter to Christ. The purpose was to get the unchurched to the crusade. Any churched member would get free transportation to the crusade—if he brought an unchurched person with him.

Extra meetings had to be scheduled, sometimes three a day. Londoners hungered for God, he kept reminding himself, not for Billy Graham. But he could show them how to find God. The Church of England quickly came into the fold. Realizing that not sponsoring Billy was a horrible blunder, they now offered their own clergy as counselors. And of course Billy gratefully welcomed their participation.

"Much more potential remains untapped," explained his hosts, who were now scrambling to maximize his message. "We're turning people away by the thousands."

So his ingenious hosts set up a network of sites, with Billy's sermon relayed to each site by telephone. Now each sermon was heard at over four hundred churches and rented halls in 175 cities in Great Britain and Ireland. At each site, the local clergy participated, talking to the audience before the sermon and counseling them afterward, just as they would have done at the arena.

On the last day of the crusade, Billy spoke to crowds of sixty-seven thousand and one hundred twenty thousand in stadiums at White City and Wembley. Between sermons, Billy was as limp as a rag with fatigue but rallied to preach strongly at Wembley. The day was such a stupendous success that the archbishop of Canterbury seemed dazed in Wembley Stadium as he murmured, "I don't think we'll ever see a sight like this again until we get to heaven."

In London, Billy had preached to two million people. Nearly forty thousand had come to the altar. Once again, as he had experienced in Boston four years earlier, he felt a compulsion to remain. On the other hand, as always, he was scheduled to go other places. Could he let those places down? And something else bothered him: Were people attracted to Billy Graham instead of Christ? If he stayed in London, didn't he risk enhancing his own image, instead of leading people to the Cross? After discussing the matter with the archbishop of Canterbury, he decided it was better to come back to England another time.

He pushed on to Scandinavia. He preached successful one-day meetings in Helsinki, Stockholm, and Copenhagen. Stockholm had a turnout of sixty-five thousand. He went on to Amsterdam to preach to forty thousand. At each stop, the Navigators followed up on the roughly 2 percent of those who attended the crusades who came to the altar to inquire. Then the European trip began to unravel in Germany. Local ministers had resisted the Navigators, automatically assuming the response to Billy's appeal would be zero.

In Dusseldorf, Billy awoke in the night with racking pain. A doctor diagnosed a kidney stone. Billy needed to rest, but he couldn't pass up his next stop: Berlin. It was too important. The symbolism was gigantic. The crusade organizers had reserved mammoth Olympic Stadium, the very stadium where Adolf Hitler had postured in 1936. And most important, the East German Communists were frantic. The Communists had launched a virulent propaganda campaign against the evangelist, accusing him of being a spy, a hypocrite who swilled alcohol and chased women. Billy couldn't back down.

"I must go ahead to Berlin," he told the team.

The pain returned with a vengeance. The only relief was a painkiller, which Billy refused to take because he feared it would make him groggy, and he couldn't preach in Olympic Stadium in a drugged stupor. That afternoon he preached to eighty thousand at Olympic Stadium, including twenty thousand East Berliners.

Billy's short, punchy sentences were ideal for a translated sermon. Thousands of Germans started to surge forward when Billy invited them to the altar. He had to act immediately. He told them the crusade team would not be able to counsel so many at once and urged them to write letters so local pastors could follow up.

A few days later in Paris, in spite of searing pain, he preached well again. His sermon was so well received that the team began planning a crusade for Paris. After that, he returned to North Carolina, where he had an operation for the kidney stone. The doctor ordered him to rest at home for six weeks. He was run down and underweight, but the results of the Berlin crusade helped speed his recovery—more than sixteen thousand letters had been sent in by inquirers.

In March 1955, Billy once again crossed the Atlantic, this time for his All-Scotland Crusade, which the churches officially supported. The support was not lukewarm, either, but steamy hot. Scotland was in the grips of a wave of evangelism among its clergy. Every reserved seat in Kelvin Hall, the site of the crusade in Glasgow, was booked solid for all six weeks.

The training of counselors reached a new high. First, about

six hundred clergy from all over Scotland came to Glasgow to take classes. Armed with certain knowledge of what was taught to the counselors, the clergy recruited members of their congregations to attend. In all, more than four thousand volunteer counselors were trained for the crusade.

Because the organizers fully expected Kelvin Hall to be full every meeting, they arranged to seat the overflow in a nearby auditorium that received a televised version of the meeting. But one element bothered him before the first meeting: His hosts warned him, "We Scots do not come to the altar. Inquirers normally wait in the back of the church or are discretely shunted into a side room."

Should Billy try his usual method? Would Scots come to Christ so publicly? Several clergy advised him not to try it. But Billy, in spite of periods of nail-biting doubt, was always a risk-taker. He took a deep breath and called them forward at the end of the first meeting. There was such a flood of Scots rushing to the altar that clergy on the platform with Billy began crying.

The crusade never wavered. The response night after night was so gratifying that the organizers expanded their crusade by telephoned broadcasts into England, Ireland, and Wales. During Easter week, the meetings were also televised and radioed to other parts of Scotland by a network far more sophisticated than the one hastily rigged at Harringay Arena the previous year.

"Are you ready for the finale?" asked Grady, trying to act nonchalant.

"If the Holy Spirit is," answered Billy nervously.

The climax was the Good Friday meeting where Billy was accessible by BBC television to virtually all of Britain. He had fretted about it for a week. People were saying only Queen Elizabeth's coronation had been watched by so many British. It was going to be watched from pubs to Buckingham Palace. All morning of Good Friday, he read and reread the Bible's four stories of the crucifixion. Christ's suffering floored him. That night, Billy was sure he spoke by the power of the Holy Spirit on the meaning of the cross.

Billy went on to England, where he held a seven-night crusade in Wembley Stadium. He was apprehensive. Was it too soon to return? His London critics seemed almost devilishly quiet, and that bothered him. He did not fill the stadium every night, and that was what the critics jumped on: the glass was half-empty. A turnout of eighty thousand became through their eyes a failure to fill all the seats.

"Stop moping, Billy. Don't forget our invitation," reminded Ruth.

"Praise God for that," agreed Billy. "I must not diminish that blessing, even if we do have to keep it a secret."

9
Christianity Today

Billy and Ruth had been invited to meet with the Queen Mother and Princess Margaret. From them, Billy learned the royal family had been following his activity very closely. They even knew details about his family life. Five days later, in strictest confidence, he was allowed to preach to young Queen Elizabeth and her retinue at Windsor Castle.

He preached on chapter 27 of Acts, building his sermon around Paul's statement of faith after the angel visited him on the sinking Alexandrian ship: "So keep up your courage, men, for I have faith in God that it will happen just as he told me."

Billy moved on to Paris for five meetings then blazed through twelve cities in Switzerland, Germany, Scandinavia, and Holland. He returned to America, then Canada, to hold a three-week crusade in Toronto.

In early 1956, Billy traveled to India. Once again, measured

Billy Graham shows his animated preaching style during his 1955 visit to Scotland. This photo was taken in Glasgow's Kelvin Hall.

by the size of the crowds he attracted, Billy was successful. But in his own mind, the trip was successful only because he recruited a man named Akbar Abdul-Haqq. Billy would bring him to America and train him to lead his own crusades in India. Turnouts of one hundred thousand, with little advance preparation, proved the Indians were receptive.

Billy made one-day stops in the Philippines, Korea, Hong Kong, Formosa, Japan, and Hawaii before returning to the United States.

It was a long, hot summer. The issue of racial injustice was simmering. Blacks no longer would submit to separate seating, water fountains, or schools—or to high poll taxes to discourage them from voting. Billy had discussed the problems with President Eisenhower, and both agreed the injustices were intolerable but that white southerners had to be nudged along. Strong-arm policies were dangerous.

> *"The hearts of bigots have to be changed first."*

"The hearts of bigots have to be changed first," warned Billy.

Billy went about it. He phoned the governors of North Carolina and Tennessee to urge them to address the racial problems from a spiritual point of view and promote justice. Then he phoned or met with prominent white and black religious leaders in the South.

His viewpoint became well-known. "If the extremists on both sides will just cool down, we can have a nice peaceful adjustment of black equality over the next ten years." Response to his moderation was swift. He was attacked from integrationists on one side and segregationists on the other.

Since Christmas 1954, Billy and his father-in-law, Nelson Bell, had talked about a magazine for evangelicals similar to *Christian Century*, the magazine liberal Christians had published for many years. Billy could never forget *Christian Century* for very long because the secular press quoted it constantly as if it were the only respectable religious publication. Though it lambasted Billy constantly, he had no thoughts of revenge. It was simply a case of fulfilling a need for evangelicals.

In fall 1955, Nelson Bell resigned his surgical practice to ramrod the magazine, already called *Christianity Today*. By the middle of 1956, Carl Henry was appointed managing editor. The first issue was scheduled for fall 1956. Billy was tempted to make the magazine the official voice of BGEA. Finally he decided that would diminish the magazine's broad appeal. Still, he served on its board.

In many ways, Billy felt *Christianity Today* was the last cog in the evangelical machine he had built, even if the magazine was semi-independent. He spread the Gospel in crusades, movies, radio, television, a newspaper column, and a book. Surely that was diverse enough. He didn't have to completely control the magazine, too. Nelson Bell and Carl Henry were as true "new evangelicals" as he was.

Some were calling Billy's movement "New Evangelicalism," an effort to distinguish it from Fundamentalism. In his heart, Billy believed Fundamentalism. Just like Fundamentalists, Billy believed that scripture was true and inspired by God; that man's original sin was true; that Christ was born of a virgin; that Christ's divinity, atonement, resurrection, and Second Coming were all true.

The problem lay with a handful of intolerant Fundamentalists who gave Fundamentalism a bad name. Billy believed men had to be tolerant of other people's beliefs. Evangelicals had to love liberal Christians and try to persuade them, not fight them. He knew there was some biblical foundation for the combative style of a few Fundamentalists like Carl McIntire. After all, Jesus had blistered the Pharisees. But Jesus usually tried to persuade His opponents. And Billy had to admit he was skeptical about some of the Fundamentalists' pugilistic attitudes that did not center on Christ's love.

"If folks want to label me a New Evangelical, that's fine with me," said Billy, who never claimed to be the founder of New Evangelicalism but knew he was the most visible.

Billy became totally absorbed in getting ready for his New York campaign in May 1957. BGEA approached the crusade with complete optimism. They contracted Madison Square Garden for several weeks.

The Protestant Council of New York, which represented thirty-one denominations and seventeen hundred churches, had presented a united front in inviting Billy in 1957. But New York was the nerve center of the rest of America, too. Billy was immediately attacked from Fundamentalists on the right and the liberal theologian Reinhold Niebuhr on the left. Their attacks seemed nitpicky, but they were unrelenting.

It was soon obvious the results in New York were going to be staggering. Night after night, Billy preached to nearly twenty thousand people. After it was clear he was going to pack the

Garden every night, BGEA approached the ABC television network to buy airtime for nationwide Saturday night specials. The first one, on June 1st, competed with television giants Jackie Gleason and Perry Como on the other two networks. Billy got only 20 percent of the total viewers. He was a distant third, yet he reached an astounding six million viewers.

BGEA began to get fifty thousand letters a week. Billy topped himself in New York week after week. He appeared as a guest on all the network news shows. Celebrities were drawn to the revivals like flies to honey: Walter Winchell, Ed Sullivan, Edward G. Robinson, John

> *BGEA began to get fifty thousand letters a week.*

Wayne, Pearl Bailey, Jack Dempsey, Sonja Henie, Dorothy Kilgallen, Gene Tierney, Greer Garson, Ethel Waters, and others.

Howard Jones, a black evangelical at BGEA, arranged for Billy to speak at a black church in Harlem. And in an inspired move, Billy invited the Reverend Martin Luther King, the black civil rights leader, to open one service at the Garden in prayer. As usual, Billy's approach to the race problems was low key. He did not harangue the audience afterward but let the notion soak in that whites and blacks work together for God. His comments in magazines were more blunt: hating anyone because of the color of his skin is a sin.

By the time the revival drew to a close, Billy had preached to more than two million people, getting fifty-five thousand inquirers for Christ. But he wasn't through yet. He drew one hundred thousand into Yankee Stadium, and for his finale, he drew two hundred thousand people into Times Square.

When Billy returned to Little Piney Cove, GiGi had left for Hampden-Dubose, a Christian boarding school in Florida. Ruth was adamant that there was too much sin in the local public school. And Ruth, at thirty-seven, was five months' pregnant.

His return home was not relaxing. The outside world would not leave him alone. Racial problems were ablaze everywhere. Even in Billy's own hometown of Charlotte, a black girl had been harassed for trying to go to all-white Harding High School. Billy quickly wrote her a letter, urging her to "hold fast and carry on. . . . You have been chosen. Those cowardly whites against you will never prosper. . . . Be of good faith. . . . [God] will see you through."[1]

Then a confrontation caught the entire nation's attention. Arkansas governor, Faubus, was going to defy the Supreme Court's 1954 ruling that schools had to desegregate. He refused to allow blacks to enter Central High School in Little Rock. On the pretext that he was preventing violence, he stationed 270 National Guardsmen at the high school.

Billy told a newspaper reporter, "It is the duty of every Christian, when it does not violate his relationship with God, to obey the law."[2] And Billy made it plain: Faubus was in the wrong. Bigotry was a sin.

What in the world could Billy do to top 1957?

10
Central America and Africa

As 1958 began, Billy toyed with the idea of establishing a college. No college emphasized the broad band of evangelicalism that Billy believed. There was no lack of enthusiasm for the idea. At the mere mention of a possible college near New York, supporters flocked to his aid: Vice President Nixon, former New York governor Thomas Dewey, radio commentator Paul Harvey. But it soon became apparent this support assumed he would be the keystone of the new school. But his experience at Northwestern Bible School taught him he was no college administrator. Nor, in his heart, did he want to be.

"Besides, it seems a little indulgent now," he confided to Ruth. "Racial injustices need to be pushed front and center."

He was already doing for that issue what he did best. Constant verbal and written attacks on him by the Ku Klux Klan and the

Billy Graham leaves the White House on March 20, 1956, after spending nearly an hour with President Dwight D. Eisenhower.

White Citizens Council proved he was hitting them where it hurt. He would attest loud and clear that bigotry was a sin. He would show support for black leaders like Martin Luther King, as long as they were pacifists. But in his heart, he knew the black leaders were doing it best. And he feared a faster pace might set the South on fire.

His cup seemed full. A second son, Nelson Edman, was born January 12th and immediately dubbed "Ned." Besides crusades, Billy had to maintain outlets in newspapers, books, radio, television, and movies. He mothered *Christianity Today* as a member of its board. He was always adding new people to his BGEA staff.

Closest to his evangelical heart, Billy worked on refining crusades. Few people appreciated how much time was actually devoted to a crusade. Praying, organizing workers, and training counselors started months ahead of the actual meetings. That part of the crusade process satisfied Billy. Actual counseling after the crusade, pioneered by Dawson Trotman, was well-known in concept but not as well executed. The real bottleneck in the evangelical process was turning the babes in Christ over to the churches. The conversions were so superficial, there was not enough time for the process to work.

The team went to Central America for three weeks, San Francisco for seven weeks, Sacramento for one week, and Charlotte for several weeks. Those crusades sprouted more opportunities. In San Francisco, Billy's message converted minister Sherwood Wirt from a devotee of liberal theology to an evangelical. Wirt was a man of many talents. With a doctorate from the University of Edinburgh, he also had once edited a newspaper. With Billy's encouragement, he wrote articles about the San Francisco crusade for *Christianity Today* then started writing a book on the crusade.

Billy's mind was cranking. "I still want a small magazine as the official voice of BGEA. Sherwood is very able."

That fall, racists bombed a high school in Clinton, Tennessee. The school had just been desegregated. Billy stepped forward to declare, "Every Christian should take his stand against these outrages." In December he spoke in Clinton to an audience of five thousand to raise money for a new school, calling, as he always did in his own heart, for "forgiveness, cool heads, and warm hearts."

One day in January 1959 when Billy was playing golf, a pain stabbed Billy's left eye.

At the Mayo Clinic, doctors discovered that Billy suffered edema in his eye. Preparation for a new crusade was well underway. The team was going to Australia and New Zealand in just a few weeks, but Billy was ordered to rest. His schedule in Australia was pared back. He rested in Hawaii with Ruth and the Grady Wilsons. But he was not idle. "This is surely God's way of making me recharge my spiritual batteries," Billy said. "Maybe I've taken Australia too lightly."

When he opened in Melbourne in February 1959, pessimists said there just wasn't enough population in Australia to mount huge crowds. But in just four weeks, Billy preached to one million Australians. He felt he was watching the power of the Holy Spirit. Billy was sure that God was at work.

Back in America, Billy held two rallies in Little Rock, where racist groups mounted hate campaigns against him. But Governor Faubus was shrewd. He urged segregationists to leave him

Billy Graham shows off his golf swing while vacationing in Puerto Rico in 1962. From there, he would begin a preaching tour through Latin America.

Billy Graham makes friends with children in western Nigeria in February 1960.

alone. And Billy, practicing the Gospel of love, talked to everyone, trying to heal Little Rock of its bitterness. At the crusade meetings, local pastors were stunned to see avowed racists coming to the altar.

At home, timid Anne was now the oldest child at eleven. Mild-mannered Bunny had just turned nine, a few weeks before Ned would turn two. Franklin was seven and seemed destined to replace GiGi as the instigator of mischief. How he loved to badger Ned! At times, Ruth was so desperate that she studied a book on training dogs. Her solutions as a parent were definitely not orthodox. Once on the way to a drive-in restaurant, she locked quarrelsome Franklin in the trunk of the car. In Asheville, he emerged from the trunk unrepentant, with the poise of a cat burglar. "I'll have a cheeseburger. Hold the onions."

Billy had decided that 1960 was going to be a year abroad. He started in Africa in January. The crusade through Africa skipped the most powerful country on the continent: South Africa. When Billy found out that blacks could not attend his rallies and that his own black evangelist Howard Jones would have problems rooming and eating there, the crusade abandoned South Africa. When those conditions could be met, he would go there.

He began in Liberia, where Howard Jones evangelized several months every year. He told them how God's Son, Jesus, had been born near Africa and how He had found refuge as a child in Africa. He was not European-looking at all but dark skinned and dark eyed. The Libyan Simon had helped Jesus carry His cross. Billy felt those connections helped the Africans open their hearts to Christ.

But for the team, the turnouts in Liberia were low, a few thousand every day. The turnouts were low in Ghana, too. In Nigeria, Billy drew large crowds, more than one hundred thousand in one week.

The Muslims had managed to have his invitation to Sudan withdrawn, so he went on to Kenya, Tanganyika, and Rhodesia. He was received with open arms in Ethiopia, a country with a Christian tradition dating back to the apostle Phillip. In Egypt, Billy learned a full-scale crusade might be possible but decided it would be too provocative in an overwhelmingly Muslim country. He visited Jordan, whose king made it clear he was being pressured into seeing him. He was not welcome.

In Israel, he was not allowed to hold public meetings. And he was warned not to so much as mention the name of Jesus to any Jew. But Billy made the most of his time. He felt he convinced influential Israeli politicians Abba Eban and Golda Meir that he was a true friend of Israel.

Ruth was very excited about Billy's next trip. In Switzerland, where Billy would crusade for one month, the entire Graham family were guests of Ara Tchividjian, a wealthy man converted through Billy's book *Peace with God*. Billy preached one-week revivals in Berne, Basal, and Lausanne. Then he preached two days in Zurich.

After Switzerland, Billy returned to Germany. The finale of a one-week crusade was right by the Brandenburg Gate in front of the old Reichstag building where the Nazis flaunted their over-sized swastika. In a huge tent, Billy preached to twenty-five thousand Germans, many from East Germany.

11
Ministering in
Turbulent Times

Billy spent the first four months of 1961 in Florida, including a three-week crusade in Miami and shorter revivals in other cities. In the spring, Fort Lauderdale's mayor appealed to Billy to calm vacationing college students. Billy had always been effective with students. In England and at Yale, he had defused students hell-bent on mocking his message. He accepted.

"What do you believe in?" he asked the crowd of several thousand partying students on the beach.

"Sex!" screamed the crowd.

"Yes, that's important. Without it, we wouldn't be here today."[1] It was that kind of good-natured reaction to taunting that won people of any age. The students listened to Billy talk about Jesus for an hour.

Billy left for England again. This time his crusade would take place in Manchester, strategically midway between London and

Glasgow, where he had previously crusaded. The crusade drew an average of thirty thousand every night—even though Billy was sick the first week. Measured against any standard but Billy's own successes, the crusade was a success. But by his standards, it was disappointing. It became etched in the team's minds like the failure at Altoona.

The team made it a model of how not to crusade. Do not campaign in a steep-staired outdoor stadium during the rainy season. Do not go where support from local churches is wavering. Do not go where the local churches try to set certain conditions and restrict the crusade. Do not hire a public relations firm from another region of the country.

Back in America, Billy crusaded during the fall in Philadelphia. The following year, he crusaded in El Paso, Chicago, and South America. The South American crusade, split into two separate campaigns, lasted a total of nine weeks. Billy blazed through the Catholic bastions of Colombia, Venezuela, Paraguay, Uruguay, Chile, Argentina, and Brazil. Every city was an adventure. Crowds, except for those in Venezuela, were small but intensely interested.

Sandwiched between the South American trips, Billy held a very successful crusade in Chicago in June, drawing forty thousand night after night to McCormick Place. At the finale at Soldier Field, he spoke to 116,000, one of his largest American audiences ever.

At the Chicago rally, twenty-seven trainees from seven different schools watched Billy and his team in action. They were bankrolled by Lowell Berry, a wealthy Californian. It seemed to

Billy Graham tests local transportation during his tour of Egypt, March 1960.

President John F. Kennedy hosts Billy Graham in the White House, December 12, 1961.

be such valuable training that Robert Ferm began to structure a formal program for El Paso later that year. Billy had always toyed with the idea of a school.

"Maybe this is the form God wants my school to take," said Billy. "On-the-job training at the 'Billy Graham School of Evangelism.'"

It was also at the Chicago rally that T.W. Wilson became Billy's right-hand man. Grady's brother could get things done faster than anyone Billy ever had on the team.

In August 1962, Billy's father died. For several years, Frank had suffered small strokes, each time surviving but a little weaker, a little shakier. Finally, one morning in the hospital, while calmly talking to his doctor, he quietly expired. Frank was seventy-four.

In September, Billy and Ruth got a letter from Stephan Tchividjian, the son of Ara Tchividjian, the man who had been their host in Switzerland. Stephan very formally asked for the hand of GiGi in marriage. He was a very mature young man studying to be a psychologist. The Grahams were not totally surprised. Stephan had shown great interest in GiGi in Switzerland.

Billy told Ruth, "Many times I have prayed for such husbands for our daughters." And he could see that Ruth was pleased, too. But who knew what GiGi thought?

Billy crusaded in El Paso in November then headed home to Little Piney Cove. By Christmas, GiGi was home from Wheaton College and Stephan Tchividjian was there, too. It seemed like no time at all before GiGi and Stephan were coordinating their wedding with Billy's crusade in France and West Germany. They were married in May 1963.

In the second half of 1963, Billy crusaded in the Los Angeles Coliseum, drawing more than 130,000 at the finale. The Billy Graham School of Evangelism was well under way. The team taught a hundred seminarians and pastors all day in classrooms. At night they all participated in the crusade.

In 1964, Texas billionaire H. L. Hunt offered to bankroll a run by Billy for the Republican nomination for President of the United States. But Billy publicly squelched the idea and resumed his crusades, the most notable of which was in Boston. This time, every meeting was at the Boston Garden with a finale at Boston Commons. Billy visited the notorious Combat Zone of sleazy bars and strip-joints and purveyors of pornography. He was cheered by the sinners.

Billy and Ruth became grandparents. Billy was just forty-five and Ruth a mere forty-three when GiGi gave birth to the first grandchild. Ruth still had six-year-old Ned at home herself! And Franklin, the most rebellious child of all five, was only eleven. Ruth seldom traveled now.

> *On Easter Sunday, Billy held a large integrated rally in Birmingham, where a black church had been bombed.*

Billy launched 1965 with a crusade in Hawaii. He followed with crusades in Copenhagen and Denver. Then, at President Lyndon Johnson's request, he visited Selma, Alabama, where there was so much racial strife that civil rights activists had been murdered.

On Easter Sunday, Billy held a large integrated rally in Birmingham, where a black church had been bombed. Thirty-five thousand, half black and half white, attended.

In late summer, Billy had one of his dark moments. It was just days before his crusade was scheduled to begin in the Astrodome in Houston, and he truly felt the Holy Spirit had deserted him. Some organizers in Houston could not understand what he meant and believed Billy had a physical problem. But those closest to him knew he really meant the Holy Spirit. Two nights before the crusade was to begin, as Billy struggled to speak to a college group, he felt the Holy Spirit return. The crusade in the Astrodome was memorable, not only for that but because it was the first one a president attended.

Billy had another book published. *World Aflame* sold a hundred thousand copies in the first three months. The title was apt for current events in America, too. Never had America seen so much rebellion. Some blacks had tired of the American process and now spouted Communist rhetoric. College students were violently opposed to fighting in Vietnam. Billy had mixed feelings about the war himself. But he realized many young people were using their rebellion as an excuse to indulge in sex and drugs. Issues became muddled and ugly.

When Billy went to England in 1966, he saw that the deterioration of spirit had gone much further there than in America. Decay was in the very heart of the church, and leading clerics simply could no longer swallow the truths of the Gospel.

By any measurement, the crusade at Earls Court Arena in

London was a success. Billy preached in person to more than one million people in only one month. Another innovation was added: closed-circuit television to ten English cities. Sharp minds had extended his revivals before 1966 by electronics, but this state-of-the-art technology yielded a production almost superior to the original. A giant screen showed Billy up close, something few saw at the real event. Billy was asked to return in 1967 and conduct another closed-circuit revival from Earls Court Arena.

Billy had encouraged the international meeting of evangelicals but refrained from organizing it under BGEA. He did not want to control it. He did little except to suggest invitations to Fundamentalists and Pentecostals so that the congress would truly be a third Christian force in the world.

12
Billy Graham Day

Back in Montreat, Anne married Danny Lotz. Bunny, fifteen, was now at Stony Brook, a boarding school in New York. So was Franklin, at fourteen. Only nine-year-old Ned was at home during the school year. Ruth was just a few years from being free to travel with Billy during the school year, although summers would be occupied with children for many years to come.

Billy went to Vietnam for Christmas. He preached twenty-five times, often combining talents with Bob Hope. Vietnam was far worse than he had thought.

In his citywide crusades, now trimmed to a Sunday-to-Sunday eight days, he started each sermon behind the pulpit, which had clocks seen only by him and guests on the platform. He always knew exactly how much time he had remaining before he invited people to the altar. His preaching had fallen into a very successful format. In his experience, people suffered from four maladies:

emptiness, loneliness, guilt, and fear of death. Unless he was aiming at a specific audience, like teenagers and how they could enlist Christ to fight sexual temptation, he would tackle one of those main four human miseries.

Billy was always very uneasy during the call to the altar. But as dozens of lost souls started to come forward for salvation, he was overwhelmed by his gift. He was so unworthy. He would plant his chin in his right hand, suddenly very self-conscious, reminding himself they were responding to the Holy Spirit, not Billy Graham. And yet when they arrived, he had to acknowledge them. He tried to make eye contact with every one of them.

He said the "Sinner's Prayer" with them:

> *Oh God, I am a sinner. I'm sorry for my sins. I'm willing to turn from my sins. I receive Christ as my Savior. I confess Him as my Lord. From this moment on, I want to follow Him and serve Him in the fellowship of the church. In Christ's name, Amen.*[1]

Then counselors took them under their wings.

The year 1967 was the first year Billy really cut back. His schedule was limited to the Earls Court follow-up and eight-day crusades in Puerto Rico, Winnipeg, Kansas City, and Tokyo. He would turn forty-nine, and he already had suffered kidney stones, hypertension, prostate surgery, an edema from stress, and many minor ailments.

For 1968, Billy had crusades scheduled for Australia, Portland,

Billy Graham preaches to American servicemen in Vietnam on December 21, 1966. Armed Forces Radio carried the sermon to soldiers throughout South Vietnam.

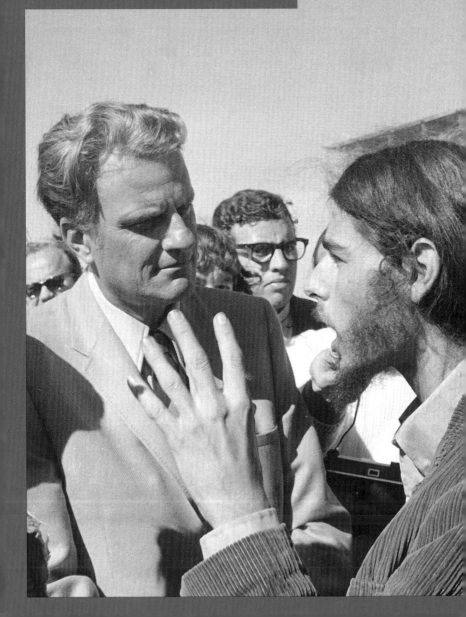

A confidant of presidents, Billy Graham could also mix with the common man. Here, he talks with young adults at the Miami-Hollywood Rock Festival in December 1969. Billy had urged the concert-goers to "turn on to God."

Pittsburgh, and San Antonio. While he was in Australia, the world turned topsy-turvy. Johnson announced he would not run again. Days later, Martin Luther King was killed by a sniper. Things did not improve after Billy returned. The virtual shoo-in for the Democratic nomination, Robert Kennedy, was assassinated in Los Angeles—just as his brother John had been assassinated five years earlier in Dallas.

Billy was heartsick at what was happening in America. He said, "America is going through its greatest crisis since the Civil War."[2]

Even Little Piney Cove was a grim reminder of how sick America had become. Although Ned was the only child still at home, life was more complicated there now. Billy was getting too many death threats. The assassinations proved the threats were all too real. Now an eleven-foot fence had to be constructed around the home at Little Piney Cove. Any approaching driver had to radio the house. Then an electronically controlled gate would open. Even at that, any visitor was greeted by bristling German shepherds, trained to explode in a split second. The protection was very depressing, even though the Grahams had been vulnerable so many years.

On the home front in 1969, Bunny married Ted Dienert, the son of the advertising executive who had pestered Billy into starting *Hour of Decision* so many years ago. All three daughters were now married, every one by the age of eighteen.

Franklin had returned home from Stony Brook in New York to finish high school in a local public school. Determined not to be a "preacher boy," he flaunted vices. He smoked cigarettes, drank alcohol, and topped his image with long hair. He rode a motorcycle and terrorized young Ned.

And Ruth warred with Franklin. One time when he overslept, she dumped his ashtray full of cigarette butts on his head. Several times she decided to win him over by showing him what a good sport she was. She hopped on his motorcycle and ran it over an embankment. Another time she rode it into a lake. The last time a split-rail fence stopped her. Billy's brothers and sisters were involved in Billy's enterprises, too. His sister Jean was married to one of BGEA's most able preachers, Leighton Ford. His sister Catherine was married to Samuel McElroy, who worked in BGEA's Charlotte office. Melvin was never officially with BGEA, but he did take the platform in the crusade at Anaheim. He told the crowd how intimidated he had been in Billy's shadow, but now he, too, had a responsibility to tell others about Jesus. And he wasn't going to stop speaking when he returned to North Carolina.

In October 1971, Charlotte held a Billy Graham Day. When first approached by the president of the Chamber of Commerce, Billy resisted. But the Chamber of Commerce played an ace in the hole. Richard Nixon liked the idea. Billy couldn't refuse the president of the United States. Nixon was superb at Billy Graham Day, speaking warmly about Billy without notes. Later, Billy was deluged with telegrams from notables like Ronald Reagan, Jimmy Stewart, Bob Hope, and Arnold Palmer. Among the guests was proud, silver-haired Morrow Graham, who still lived in the family home, surrounded not by cows and green fields but sprawling franchises and office buildings.

Billy finally held a meeting in South Africa. For years, he had refused to hold a revival in South Africa unless all South Africans were allowed to attend in unrestricted seating. The government acquiesced in 1973. The crowd of forty-five thousand at Durban's Kings Park was completely integrated. South African blacks were crying with joy. They hailed Billy's influence.

Two months later, he campaigned in South Korea. Korea was 10 percent Christian, and his host committee was wildly optimistic. They were going to stage the meetings on a former air strip, now called People's Plaza, a ribbon of concrete that stretched for one mile. But apprehensions about overreaching soon disappeared. The first service drew five hundred thousand South Koreans. As always, Billy's short, punchy sentences were ideal for translation. And to make the event attain near-perfection, the translator, a South Korean trained at Bob Jones University, was a magnificent preacher himself.

> *The first service drew five hundred thousand South Koreans.*

By the finale, expectations for a huge turnout were extremely high. But the crowd exceeded those expectations. Never had there been a crowd like this for a religious service. Its respectful silence made the attendance of 1,100,000 even harder to believe. In five days, Billy had preached to three million South Koreans.

13
Struggles, Trials, and Triumphs

The summer of 1973 was a sad, dismal one for the Grahams. In August, Nelson Bell, eighty and diabetic, passed away. He was buried in Swannanoa. Ruth's mother, Virginia, clung to life, her voice gone from a stroke.

The summer of 1974 was also a difficult one for Billy, but for different reasons. On August 9th, President Nixon resigned in the wake of the Watergate Scandal. The Watergate committee had found indisputable proof on the tapes that Nixon endorsed a cover-up. Billy, who knew and supported Nixon, tried to call him and console him, but he would not take his calls.

Some critics wanted to tar and feather Billy with Nixon, inferring that he was an insider. The irony was that Billy had been closer to President Johnson, who had invited him to the White

Billy and Ruth Graham escort actress and singer Ethel Waters to the White House wedding of President Richard Nixon's daughter Tricia in June 1971.

Billy Graham looks on as President Lyndon B. Johnson speaks outside of the White House, June 16, 1967.

House twenty-three times, five of those for overnight. Billy's visits to Nixon in the White House had been fewer. Johnson had Billy to Camp David twice; Nixon had Billy there once. And Johnson had invited Billy to the LBJ Ranch, too. The truth was that Billy knew more of the inner workings of Johnson's White House than Nixon's. But as usual, Billy ignored slander and innuendoes.

In October, Billy crusaded in South America. Ruth took the opportunity to visit GiGi and the grandchildren. While in Brazil, Billy got a phone call from GiGi. Ruth was in the hospital.

"What happened?" he cried.

"She rigged up a pipe slide for the children," explained GiGi. Billy knew a pipe slide was a short section of pipe on a wire strung at a steep angle between two trees. The slider gripped the pipe and careened down the wire. "She tried it first to make sure it was safe for the children," continued GiGi. "It wasn't safe. The wire broke and she fell fifteen feet."

"Anything broken?"

"Broken heel, cracked rib, and crushed vertebra," said GiGi sadly.

"How is she taking it? Let me talk to her."

"I'm sorry. She also has a concussion." GiGi hesitated. "She's in a coma."

Oh God, prayed Billy, *don't take Ruth yet.*

Ruth regained consciousness, but her memory was a shambles. *What else can go wrong?* thought Billy. As if he were being punished for his lack of trust, Ruth's mother died. But of course he knew he had nothing to do with it. Virginia Bell was buried in Swannanoa next to Nelson. Ruth could barely stand on crutches at the funeral. Billy felt so sad for Ruth. Here she was, trying to recover from her foolishness, and now she had lost both parents. Thank God, at least she didn't have to worry about Franklin. That summer in Switzerland and the Holy Land, the Lord had become real to Franklin. He had accepted Jesus as his Lord. Billy knew it was real, too.

Over the weeks, Ruth recovered her memory. But her hip was deteriorating, possibly from the accident. The doctors said hip surgery loomed somewhere in her future.

BGEA had two major successes in 1975 away from the crusade circuit. World Wide Pictures made its most professional film, *The Hiding Place,* about the heroic ten Boom family of Holland. They hid Jews and other refugees during World War II at a heavy price: imprisonment in Nazi death camps. The lone survivor of the family, spunky eighty-three-year-old Corrie ten Boom, attended the premiere. Corrie was a prime example of an itinerant evangelist, still living out of a suitcase, preaching the Gospel.

For a while that fall, Billy's book called *Angels* became the bestselling nonfiction hardcover. Billy wrote it because he could hardly believe there was no modern book on such a heavenly creation as angels.

In March of 1976, while crusading in Las Vegas, Billy got a shock. Grady Wilson, who over the years had ballooned to 235 pounds, suffered a massive heart attack back in North Carolina. Billy rushed east. At the hospital, the doctor said no one could visit Grady in intensive care.

"Doctor," Billy said calmly, "I'm going into Grady's room, and I'm going in now." And he entered the room to pray at Grady's side. Of all the team members, Grady was closest to Billy. He was Billy's sidekick, and the one who kicked him in the seat of the pants when his nose was too high in the air.

Grady recovered, and Billy soon had little time to think about anything but his own reputation. In spring 1977, the Charlotte newspaper, the *Observer,* ran a very detailed series on the financial structure of BGEA. Billy had fed them information himself, right on the porch of Little Piney Cove. The BGEA was a large organization to be sure, but it was clean. Every year the organization spent as much money as it collected. And collections were low-key, never threatening or hysterical pandering or promising great prosperity.

BGEA had several hundred employees in Minneapolis. Its two buildings had modest histories. One was a three-story office building bought many years ago from an oil company. Its neighbor was once a parking garage. The board of directors had more

> *All decisions had to be approved by an executive committee made up of outside directors who did not receive payments from BGEA.*

than twenty members, both inside and outside the BGEA. The secret to BGEA's financial integrity was that all decisions had to be approved by an executive committee made up of outside directors who did not receive payments from BGEA. The outside directors were all seasoned executives of other companies. As far back as 1960, the executive committee had set up a trust for all the royalties from Billy's books—at the time a mere two books, but by 1977 six books with sales in the millions of copies. A bank administered the trust, directing money to BGEA or other charities.

Like any institution, BGEA had critics. Some complained about the generous pension plans for workers in BGEA. Some complained about the annuities solicited by BGEA. But Billy had been extra cautious even with those. The principal behind the annuity was always completely protected during the lifetime of the contributor. So in the unlikely case BGEA ever went bankrupt, the annuity contributors would get every nickel of the principal back. And BGEA refused to invest in public stocks, so as not to appear to endorse any corporation or product.

As Billy finished reading the final installment of the series, he sighed. "The Charlotte *Observer* concluded BGEA is squeaky clean and had the decency to say so."

But as careful as Billy had been with his financial dealings and disclosing them, in summer 1977, the *Observer* screamed betrayal and hypocrisy. The investigative reporters who wrote the series for the *Observer* discovered there was another organization connected with Billy that did not spend all the money it collected but had amassed more than twenty million dollars—and that was invested heavily in public stock. The World Evangelism and Christian Education Fund (WECEF) was incorporated in Dallas. Nine of its eleven board members were also board members of

BGEA. The other two were Ruth and her brother Clayton!

"Why didn't they ask me about that before they attacked me in their paper?" lamented Billy. "Now it looks like I was hiding something."

Billy now had to devote much time to defending himself. He had to explain on the *Hour of Decision* that WECEF was a separate organization set up to promote three missions. It was to establish in Asheville a training center for laymen. Secondly, it was to start a training center for evangelism connected with Wheaton College. Thirdly, it funded the youth programs: Campus Crusade, the Fellowship of Christian Athletes, and Young Life. Why did WECEF have such a surplus of money? Because the first two missions would require such funds when construction actually started. And WECEF was no secret. Billy had announced its creation in Minneapolis in 1970.

Later Billy remembered that as recently as 1976, he had discussed it candidly with a reporter from another newspaper in the same chain that owned the *Observer*. The reporter had not used the material, but he had taped the conversation. When the *Observer* was informed of this and still refused to retract their accusations, Billy managed to get the tape released to the Associated Press. They printed the truth about the situation, and many editorials scolded the *Observer* for deliberately not setting the record straight.

Billy thought he had been careful with money matters, but he realized now he had to be even more so. Billy immediately set about to organize a council that would hold evangelical organizations accountable for the way they handled money. It was time to put a stop to the growing image of money-grubbing evangelicals.

Later in 1977, Billy met with Alex Haraszti, an evangelical surgeon in Atlanta. Haraszti was a naturalized American who had immigrated from Hungary to escape Communism.

Haraszti asked, "How would you like to hold a full-fledged crusade in Hungary?"

"A crusade for Christ in a Communist country? What a question. Of course I would!"

Haraszti explained that America had two things Hungary wanted. Since the end of World War II, the American army had held Hungary's most precious religious symbol, the Crown of St. Stephen, Hungary's patron saint. America refused to return it, claiming Hungary's current government was not legitimate, that it was no more than a puppet controlled by the Soviets. And secondly, the current government in Hungary wanted "most-favored-nation" trade status with America.

"But how can we deliver these things?" asked Billy nervously. "Those things can only be obtained at the highest level of government." Was Haraszti going to ask Billy to use his influence with Jimmy Carter?

"Leave it to me," Haraszti said.

Haraszti launched his plan, as intricate as an espionage thriller, to get Billy's crusade into Hungary. By late 1977, Billy opened his crusade in a church in Budapest. The few hundred Hungarians there were not only nervous, they were mildly hostile. Why was this happening? But as always, Billy's preaching won their hearts. The hostility turned into anticipation then love. By the end of the ten days, he had preached several times, once to a crowd of thirty thousand. He also met with Jewish leaders and government officials.

The Hungarian triumph seemed to break down the barriers to the eastern European countries. Apparently the word spread at the highest levels. Billy was not dangerous. He might even satiate the populace's hunger for God, which never seemed to go away. The following year Billy preached in Poland.

In 1979, Billy finally saw the formation of the organization called the Evangelical Council for Financial Accountability (ECFA). Membership in ECFA would be voluntary. But he knew one organization that would join and would strictly adhere to its guidelines: BGEA.

Later that year, Billy went to Red China with Ruth, her brother Clayton, and her sisters, Rosa and Virgina. They visited the old family mission in Tsingkiang. Ruth had tried to arrange the trip for years. The trip had finally been expedited by none other than Richard Nixon, who had remained a friend of Billy's. They had reconciled several months after Nixon's resigna-

The China trip was far more than a trip into nostalgia.

tion. The China trip was far more than a trip into nostalgia. Billy had been briefed on which officials he had to convince if he ever hoped to crusade in China. And Billy met with them, patiently explaining that Christians were good citizens, illustrating with

Romans 13 that the Bible instructed Christians to obey authorities. Billy took the officials right through the Ten Commandments on up to the pinnacle of moral perfection, the Sermon on the Mount. Now Billy would just have to go home and wait for God's will to be done.

In Charlotte, Billy's mother was now bedridden, struck down by a series of strokes. Many times she quoted to Billy the verses from 2 Timothy that she and Franklin Graham had prayed in Billy's behalf for many years: "Do your best to present yourself to God as one approved, a workman who does not need to be ashamed and who correctly handles the word of truth." His mother still prayed for him, and it was a great comfort to Billy to know that such a good heart was constantly appealing to God in his behalf.

At first his mother dreaded being helpless and looking frayed and confused. But she said she realized Satan was tempting her to complain. Finally, she comforted herself with Psalm 34: "The angel of the LORD encamps around those who fear him, and he delivers them." And more than once she described angelic beings around her bed.

In August 1981, Morrow Graham, nearly ninety years old, passed away.

"I never felt more mortal," Billy said, now sixty-two. Was he, too, winding down at long last? What was left for him to accomplish?

14
Fight the Bullies

But it was just one of Billy's dark moments.

Doors kept opening.

Billy met with the Pope for the first time. John Paul II seemed to have a special interest in Billy. In 1978, Billy had established a real rapport with the Catholic clerics in Poland. Word must have filtered back to the Pope, who was from Poland, that Billy was a serious advocate for Christ, speaking with much moral authority. They discussed relations among the great Christian movements, the rise of evangelicalism, and how Christians should respond to moral issues.

Billy felt the onset of the third great goal of his life. The first had been his commitment to preach the Gospel of Jesus Christ, the second to the elimination of racial injustice, and the third to world peace. And world peace could never be attained without dealing with Communism. Billy's most immediate goal was to crusade into the very center of Communism. He refused to think of it as having a heart, only a center.

Once again it was the uncanny shrewdness of Alex Haraszti that brought it about. Who else could spar with a Machiavellian heavyweight like the Russian ambassador Drobynin? Certainly Billy couldn't. He didn't even try but deferred to Haraszti at every turn. The result was the arrival of Billy in Moscow in May 1982—to preach the Gospel of Jesus Christ!

Jumpy diplomats at the American State Department urged him privately not to go, hinting President Reagan was very much against it. Newspapers reported that Reagan was opposed. The Sunday before Billy was to leave, he was invited to lunch with Vice President George Bush. After Billy's arrival, the Reagans showed up. The president pulled him aside, assuring Billy he must go to Russia.

In Moscow, after a series of changes imposed by very thin-skinned Communists who were determined that Billy would not draw a large crowd of Russians, he preached at a church, unannounced, very early on a Sunday morning. The sermon still drew an audience of one thousand. The Communists intercepted others trying to get there, and kept them behind barricades several blocks away. But Billy was delighted.

"We've made a real start for Christ," he told Haraszti.

Several people used the occasion to make public protests of Communist injustice. Billy brushed them off. He had to restrain himself from sympathizing publicly, or he would never be allowed to return. Patience was always one of his virtues.

The secular press magnified every gaffe Billy made in Russia.

Billy Graham accompanies President Ronald Reagan for a May 3, 1987, speech at New York's Ellis Island.

When Billy spoke of religious freedom in Russia in the hope it would come about, the press chided him for being a backward rube, a dupe of the Russians. Billy just told himself the attacks were not personal.

For a long time, Billy had wanted a world conference for evangelicals who were really out there preaching to sinners. Earlier congresses at Berlin and Lausanne dealt with matters far more abstract than being heckled on a street corner. Now he wanted a conference that instructed evangelists on how to compose sermons, how to draw crowds, how to raise money, how to use videos, and every other aspect of day-to-day evangelizing. The conference held in Amsterdam in 1983 was called the International Conference for Itinerant Evangelists, or ICIE. It drew nearly four thousand preachers from one hundred countries. Their tales were both encouraging and heart-breaking. One Kenyan had seen only 130 people converted in ten years. That was too typical. And some preachers were so poor that they collected empty plastic cups and trays at the conference to take back with them. They couldn't bear to see such wonderful utensils wasted.

During the early 1980s, Billy held crusades in Canada, Japan, Mexico, and England as well as Anaheim, Anchorage, Baltimore, Boston, Boise, Chapel Hill, Fort Lauderdale, Harford, Houston, Oklahoma City, Orlando, San Jose, Spokane, and Tacoma. He never minimized the effects of any of these efforts, his main calling. But one crusade was very special to him. In September 1984, Billy finally got his first full-fledged crusade in Russia.

Billy was allowed to preach over twelve days in four cities:

Moscow, Leningrad, Novosibirsk, and Tallinin in Estonia. If the trip was not momentous enough for Billy, there was an added benchmark. His son, Franklin, newly ordained, preached with him.

In 1986, Amsterdam again hosted the International Congress of Itinerant Evangelists. This time, ICIE drew more than nine thousand evangelists, many brought there at the expense of BGEA. Some stories were coming back about the results of the previous conference. Some evangelists were having staggering successes now.

> *His son, Franklin, newly ordained, preached with him.*

The ICIE also hatched a plan of staggering proportions. With transmission of television now possible by communication satellites circling the globe, a program could be beamed to many portable receiving stations all around the world—even in remote areas, as long as they could find a large enough audience to justify it. They began to plan an enormous network of receiving stations radiating from Billy's live London crusade in English and from his live Latin American crusade in English/Spanish. They would call it "Mission World."

In 1986, Billy also held a Greater Washington, D.C., Crusade, the first one in which he rigorously enlisted help from black churches from the outset. Other crusades followed in Columbia, South Carolina, Denver, Tallahassee, and abroad in France and Helsinki. A crusade in China was now deemed possible.

And yet, 1987 was a year of infamy for American evangelists.

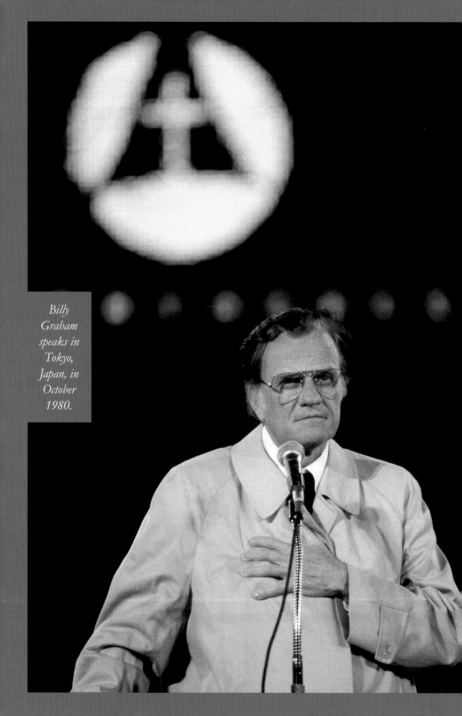

Billy Graham speaks in Tokyo, Japan, in October 1980.

Billy felt helpless as he watched evangelism tainted by immorality, dishonesty, and bizarre behavior. The first blow came when his old friend Oral Roberts solicited funds on television by saying that God told him he would be taken to heaven if several million dollars were not raised for Oral's medical school in Tulsa. The second blow came when Jimmy Bakker of PTL (Praise the Lord) Ministries was scandalized when it became known he paid hush money to a church secretary with whom he'd had an affair. PTL, already very shaky financially, was revealed as a fiasco, promising contributors accommodations at their resort, Heritage USA—accommodations that didn't exist. Bakker and his wife were drawing annual salaries and bonuses totaling over one million dollars as the PTL ministry was going bankrupt. The third blow came when popular televangelist Jimmy Swaggart, who had self-righteously condemned Bakker publicly, was discovered with a prostitute in Metairie, Louisiana.

All these scandals were outdone by a great personal loss for Billy. Grady Wilson had been suffering from heart trouble for ten years. His activity had tailed off, but he still attended some of Billy's crusades. The Pillsbury Doughboy face couldn't be missed. Joy seemed to radiate away from it.

Yet everyone, including Grady, seemed to realize his stay in the hospital in fall 1987 was going to be his last. His unwavering cheery attitude proved to everyone how deep his faith was. At the funeral, Billy told what a great inspiration Grady's first sermon had been to him.

Billy always regretted how he overshadowed his cronies. He

never felt more regret than at Grady's funeral. Grady had been a fine preacher. And he was the one who loosened up worriers like Lyndon Johnson and Richard Nixon with his barrage of humor. Besides Grady's contributions, his brother T.W. was a wonderful organizer and expediter. Cliff Barrows was not only a song leader but a first-rate producer. It was Cliff who ramrodded the radio and television shows.

The press heaped scorn on televangelists. Even Billy's BGEA, which could not be considered an organization of televangelism at all, suffered. Billy's television specials were held four times a year, and he did not ask for money. He asked for hearts and souls. But many television news anchors tarred and feathered him with the others. As usual, Billy did not cry "foul."

Beyond America, the world was changing. The Berlin Wall came down. Russian leader Gorbachev, lauding new policies of restructuring Russia called "perestroika" and openness called "glasnost," appeared to be sincere.

And Billy achieved another goal: a crusade in Red China. He and Ruth, a "daughter of China," got a rousing welcome in the Great Hall of the People in Beijing. From there, Billy began a five-city crusade. He was cautious. As he had done previously in Communist countries, he emphasized that Christians were model citizens, that they should not be feared or persecuted. Second, he reassured Chinese Christians that they were part of a worldwide community of one billion Christians. Third, he pointed out that men must be at peace with God as well as the rest of mankind. Billy spent one hour with Premier Li Peng. On the way back to

Billy Graham speaks to some ten thousand people in front of Berlin, Germany's Reichstag building, March 10, 1990.

America, Billy was a guest of the Russian Orthodox Church in Moscow.

In 1989, he preached in Hungary again, this time in a stadium full of one hundred thousand nominal Communists. And his massive outreach called Mission World through satellite hookups was launched. From London, he spoke live to Britain, Ireland, and ten African countries. Delayed broadcasts were received by another twenty-three African countries. In late 1990, Mission World eventually reached millions in Asia from Billy's live crusade in Hong Kong. Some were saying it reached one hundred million viewers.

He told a reporter, "I feel like I'm ready to go to heaven. I never dreamed I would see a crusade like this." And he realized that he was echoing the archbishop of Canterbury's words thirty-four years earlier.

At home, Billy followed up crusades of New Jersey and New York with a massive rally in Central Park. How could he ever top the Times Square rally of 1957? Yet, at the age of seventy-two, he did. The rally in New York's Central Park drew two hundred fifty thousand. His peaks seemed to never end. In November, he was in Buenos Aires preaching another chapter of Mission World, which relayed his sermons throughout Latin America.

> *The rally in New York's Central Park drew two hundred fifty thousand.*

In 1992, the organization Billy helped to found, the Evangelical Council for Financial Responsibility, or ECFR, showed how truly independent it was. It censured Franklin Graham for his activities with Samaritan's Purse and World Medical Mission, claiming that he was overpaid, that he used their aircraft for private use, and that he pocketed large donations for himself. Billy and Ruth advised Franklin to withdraw his organizations from the ECFR then reapply with his defense well documented. He did—with successful results.

For five days at the end of March, Billy penetrated the most recalcitrant Communist country in the world: North Korea. The leader was Kim Il Sung. As usual, Billy began by reassuring the leader that Christians were excellent citizens: sober, obedient, and industrious.

Over the years, Billy had dealt with many illnesses: kidney stones, hernias, ulcers, tumors, polyps, hypertension, pneumonia, prostate trouble, and broken ribs. He didn't hide his complaints, either. With his usual frankness, he discussed them and didn't mind if his listener offered sympathy. He didn't get much from Ruth. But during the summer of 1992, even Ruth was stunned when Billy received the diagnosis of his latest affliction.

Billy Graham's crusades were so popular that attendees sometimes had to watch a video feed from overflow areas. This image is from Billy's final crusade, June 2005 in Queens, New York.

15
Reflecting on Retirement

"Parkinson's Disease!" gasped Ruth.

Billy's symptoms of the progressive nervous disorder were tremors in his hands and fatigue. "God comes with greater power when we are weak," answered Billy to anyone who implied he should retire.

But he had to pause and reflect. His father, Frank, a non-smoking teetotaler who worked hard, lived to be seventy-four. Grandpa Crook Graham, a hardworking heavy drinker, lived to be seventy. Grandpa Ben Coffey, more like Frank in his habits, lived to be seventy-three.

Billy was seventy-three. Even Ruth was impressed with the implications of the family tree. Billy decided he would slow down, just a bit. After all, he not only had nineteen grandchildren, but he had five great-grandchildren.

He returned to Russia in October 1992. Finally, he could

carry out a full-scale, citywide crusade. The eternal optimists of BGEA had reserved Moscow's indoor Olympic Stadium, which could hold fifty thousand. Turnouts averaged forty-five thousand. The last night drew fifty thousand, with twenty thousand standing outside. The number of inquirers was much higher than the usual two percent. It ran up to 25 percent. Cliff Barrows did not play the usual music; it only made the Russians flock to the altar dangerously fast.

> *BGEA had reserved Moscow's indoor Olympic Stadium, which could hold fifty thousand.*

"Please walk. Don't run," pleaded Billy.

In March 1993, Billy again preached over an extensive satellite network, this time from Essen, Germany. The effort was now eight years old, and it was not just an attempt to reach millions upon millions of listeners. They had learned long ago that follow-up was critical. If counselors were not there to help inquirers, the effort was largely in vain. They now had to aim not so much at how many people they could reach but how many they could reach where counseling was at hand. The new direction called for a new name: Global Mission.

The mastermind of the satellite network, Bob Williams, muttered, "But we are just now learning to do it right."

Evangelizing continued by radio, television specials in prime time, satellite networking, magazines, movies, and citywide crusades like the one in Pittsburgh that summer. Billy had books generating royalties. And new evangelists were being trained all the time in America and abroad.

In 1994, Billy ventured into the Far East again. His four-day Tokyo crusade was the best ever in Japan for BGEA. He followed that success with ten days of preaching in Red China. Then he returned to North Korea. He delivered a message to Park Il Sung from President Bill Clinton, who could make himself available when he needed a favor. This time Billy was allowed to preach in North Korea.

His citywide crusades in America were taking on a new flavor. He still preached as always but now supplemented the crusade with Youth Nights, characterized by Christian rock music. Notable was Franklin's entry in preaching at the citywide crusades. Billy knew that would cause speculation that Franklin was about to take over the helm of BGEA. And someday Franklin *would* take over—but not yet.

In March 1995, Bob Williams implemented his latest version of Global Mission. From San Juan, Billy's three nights of sermons went to thirty satellites that sent them on to 185 countries. Only Red China did not participate. The telecasts were not intended to be live. Billy's thirty-minute sermons were translated into 116 languages and augmented by local gospel musicians and testimonials. Then tapes tailored to regional audiences were shown in three thousand sites with ten million seats. One million counselors were there waiting for the inquirers as they responded to the message of Christ. The effort did not end there. The tapes were to be shown to more and more sites in the months ahead.

In June 1995, Billy collapsed at a luncheon in Toronto just before the five-day crusade was to begin. At seventy-six, he seemed constantly reminded of his mortality. Billy's friends were falling one by one. Just the year before, he had spoken at Richard Nixon's funeral. Grady was gone. Cliff Barrows and Bev Shea had lost their wives. In Toronto, doctors discovered Billy was anemic due to a loss of blood. Cancer was ruled out. He recovered enough to preach at the fourth night of the crusade to a turnout of 73,500, the largest crowd ever at the Skydome.

In moments of exhaustion, Billy reflected on retiring. He felt fulfilled. Only God knew how many people he had preached to one way or another. The BGEA in Minneapolis was healthy, and his school for evangelism at Wheaton was going strong. His center at Asheville was developing, even with the final resting place for Billy and Ruth already set aside. *Christianity Today* was a strong voice for evangelicals. His books numbered over a dozen with over ten million copies sold. More than any evangelist in history, he had fulfilled the "Great Commission" expressed by Jesus Himself in Matthew 28:19: "'Therefore go and make disciples of all nations, baptizing them in the name of the Father and of the Son and of the Holy Spirit.'"

And yet there were billions of souls out there to be saved. One of his fellow travelers he admired most also had reflected on retiring in tired and sickly moments: crusty old Dutch evangelist Corrie ten Boom. But she never did retire. She continued preaching the Gospel until her third stroke felled her at ninety-one.

So Billy, in failing health, continued to evangelize. As he had said

Former president Bill Clinton shared the stage on the second night of Billy Graham's final crusade, held in June 2005 in Queens, New York.

so many times, "I'll keep opening doors. God will sort it all out."

After the turn of the millennium, Billy—who was becoming more and more frail due to a variety of medical issues—continued his crusade ministry until June 2005. It was then, at the age of eighty-six, that he held his final meetings at Flushing Meadows Park in New York City. In the years between 2000 and 2011, he authored five additional books and updated his autobiography, *Just As I Am*. His final book, *Nearing Home: Life, Faith, and Finishing Well*, was published in 2011.

In 2000, Billy's son William Franklin Graham III was named chief executive officer of the BGEA. The following year, Franklin succeeded his father as president of the association. In 2005, after Billy's final crusade, he retired from public speaking and began spending nearly all of his time with Ruth at their home in Montreat, though Billy remained involved in the work and planning of the BGEA.

> *On June 14, 2007, Billy's beloved Ruth passed into eternity*

On June 14, 2007, Billy's beloved Ruth passed into eternity after a long battle with health issues. She had been diagnosed with spinal meningitis in 1995, and in her final months had contracted pneumonia. On June 11, at her own request and after consulting with the family, Ruth's doctors removed her from life support. She died three days later at the Graham's Little Piney Cove in Montreat with Billy and their five children at her side. She was eighty-seven.

The day before Ruth's death, Billy Graham issued an emotional statement through the BGEA: "Ruth is my soul mate and best friend, and I cannot imagine living a single day without her by my side. I am more and more in love with her today than when we first met over sixty-five years ago as students at Wheaton College."

In more than six decades of marriage, Billy and Ruth had five children, nineteen grandchildren, thirty-eight great grandchildren.

Ruth Graham received great credit for her support of Billy in his career as the world's best-known evangelist. As T. W. Wilson once said, "There would have been no Billy Graham as we know him today had it not been for Ruth. They have been a great team."[1]

And now they have both received their heavenly reward.

Four generations of Graham men celebrate Billy's ninetieth birthday in November 2008: from left to right, Billy's son Franklin; Billy; grandson Will; and great-grandson Quinn.

Epilogue

The Bible teaches that those who faithfully serve the Lord Jesus Christ on earth will receive rewards, or "crowns," on the day they meet their Master face-to-face in heaven.

One of those rewards is the "crown of rejoicing," which the apostle Paul wrote about: "For what is our hope, or joy, or crown of rejoicing? Is it not even you in the presence of our Lord Jesus Christ at His coming?" (1 Thessalonians 2:19 NKJV). This reward has also been called the "soul-winner's crown," and it honors those who made bringing others to Christ their life's work.

When "soul-winners" come to mind, it's almost impossible to avoid the name of the Rev. Billy Graham, who celebrated his ninety-fifth birthday with family and friends on November 7, 2013.

Billy Graham preached the wonderful news of salvation through Jesus Christ to more people than anyone in history. In more than sixty years of ministry, Billy preached the Gospel to an estimated 2.2 *billion* people, both through personal appearances and radio and television broadcasts. His live audiences numbered almost 215 million people in 185 countries and territories worldwide.

At the Billy Graham Crusades alone, an estimated 3.2 million souls have responded to Billy's invitations to accept Jesus as their personal savior. And only God knows how many have responded to his broadcasts and writings.

Though his impact for Christ is incalculable, one thing is certain: this farmer's son didn't see himself as anything special—he was just a man blessed enough to be called and empowered by God to proclaim the greatest message of all time.

Billy Graham would have been the first to say it wasn't his charm or ability to speak—both of which were considerable—that made him such a great evangelist. Rather, it was the empowering of God's Holy Spirit and Billy's willingness to tap into that power that allowed him to preach with such persuasiveness.

Like the faithful servant Jesus described in a parable, Billy Graham will no doubt be welcomed into heaven with the greeting, "Well done, thou good and faithful servant!"

By any measure we can think of, Billy Graham's has been a life well lived.

Welder Shaun Thorn assembles a model of a Billy Graham statue being assembled for the Southern Baptist Convention in Nashville, Tennessee. Appropriately, the statue includes both a Bible and the cross of Jesus Christ.

Notes

CHAPTER 9

1. From *A Prophet with Honor* by William Martin. Copyright 1991 by William Martin. By permission of William Morrow & Co., Inc., 245.
2. Ibid., 246.

CHAPTER 11

1. John Pollock, *Billy Graham: The Authorized Biography* (McGraw-Hill, 1966), 234.

CHAPTER 12

1. From *A Prophet with Honor* by William Martin. Copyright 1991 by William Martin. By permission of William Morrow & Co., Inc., 30.
2. Ibid., 351.

CHAPTER 15

1. From "Ruth Graham Dies at 87" by Marshall Shelley. *Christianity Today.* http://www.christianitytoday.com/ct/2007/juneweb-only/124-43.0.html